God Save the Queen?

Johann Hari

ICON BOOKS

Published in the UK in 2002
by Icon Books Ltd., Grange Road,
Duxford, Cambridge CB2 4QF
E-mail: info@iconbooks.co.uk
www.iconbooks.co.uk

Published in Australia in 2002
by Allen & Unwin Pty. Ltd.,
PO Box 8500,
83 Alexander Street,
Crows Nest, NSW 2065

Sold in the UK, Europe, South Africa
and Asia by Faber and Faber Ltd.,
3 Queen Square, London WC1N 3AU
or their agents

Distributed in Canada by
Penguin Books Canada,
10 Alcorn Avenue, Suite 300,
Toronto, Ontario M4V 3B2

Distributed in the UK, Europe,
South Africa and Asia by
Macmillan Distribution Ltd.,
Houndmills, Basingstoke RG21 6XS

ISBN 1 84046 401 1

Typesetting by Hands Fotoset

Printed and bound in the UK by
Cox & Wyman Limited, Reading

THE AUTHOR

Johann Hari graduated with a double-first in Social and Political Science from King's College, Cambridge. He now writes weekly for the *New Statesman* magazine as part of a distinguished staff body which includes John Pilger, Nick Cohen, Cristina Odone, Darcus Howe and John Lloyd. He has also written for many of Britain's leading newspapers, including the *Guardian*, the *Evening Standard* and the *Independent on Sunday*. His work has appeared in international newspapers from *El Mundo* to the *Melbourne Age*, and his revelations about Prince William became front-page news in *Le Monde*.

His first play, *Going Down in History*, was considered 'excellent' by the *Telegraph*'s theatre critic, Charles Spencer, who described him as 'the new David Hare'.

Contents

PART I

FEEDING THE BEAST

How the Monarchy Has Destroyed the Lives of the Windsor Family

Monarchists are torturing the very people they claim to love and respect. Every member of the Windsor family has been fed at birth into the sausage-machine of The Monarchy, and it has pulled and tugged and stamped at them until they are Monarch-Shaped. In the process, they have become deeply damaged human beings. This book will show how *every* Windsor has been subjected to inhuman and degrading treatment which would never be accepted if it were forced upon a 'normal' citizen.

In royal circles, they refer to the sacrifices they are forced to make for the monarchy as 'feeding the beast'. I will, first of all, show just how painful that feeding frenzy has been, and, secondly, ask whether the institution of monarchy is a beast worth feeding at all.

But before we begin that painful journey, I need to tell you a little bit about how I came to be writing this book. In January 2002, I wrote a cover story for the *New Statesman* which surmised, on the basis of evidence already in the public domain, that William Windsor does not want to be King. I drew only on very reputable sources, and my editors and I had confidence that we could make this sensational set of revelations stand up. The story caused a small ripple: *Le Monde* ran it on their cover, with the headline 'L'affaire William'; the *Daily Mail* cheekily ran on their cover a story headed 'The Boy Who Would (rather not) Be King', without crediting me as a source; and so on, for a week or so. I thought the story had run its course, and I shut royal affairs out of my mind.

Three weeks later, I met (through a mutual friend) a person who is unquestionably particularly close to William. He was very eager to know 'how I had found out', though he didn't say quite *what* he thought I had found out. I was of course cagey and deliberately ambiguous, hoping to give the impression that I knew more than I did in the hope that he would inadvertently reveal some interesting facts. It swiftly became clear that in William's closest social circle, there is a frenzied debate about whether William wants to be King, and he was only talking about his real plans to a select few. My contact explained, 'There's only one of about ten people who can have talked to you. With everybody else, he avoided the topic. But with us, he's always been very honest that being King is the last thing he wants. So which one of the ten was it? Was it—', and then he began to reel off a few names, none of which I knew.

I blabbered something about not revealing my sources and then chuntered to a halt. I was obviously very intrigued by what I was being told, but somehow I had to act very calm, as though I'd heard it all before. Clearly, this source had assumed that somebody was blabbing to me – how could I use this? Hmmm.

Then, for reasons which I still don't understand, I suddenly used the bluntest (and most ridiculously unrealistic) instrument in my armoury. I tried to calm my heartbeat and asked ever-so-sweetly if, maybe, perhaps, ummmm, William himself would be interested in talking to me, off the record? He paused. In those beautiful, precious seconds, I had visions of writing 'William: His True Story', and reaping an Andrew Morton-sized fortune to go with it.

'I'll find out', he said. 'But don't hold your breath.' Then it all went quiet again.

I rushed about working on other stories, as usual, for the next month, and gradually lost hope. One day, I was in our offices, in the middle of talking on the telephone to a radical plastic surgeon who believes he can give people wings (it was for an article; I don't want wings myself), when my mobile began to vibrate. I glanced at the screen: it was William's close friend. I hung up without even saying goodbye.

'Hi, it's [name deleted]', he said in that odd, semi-cockney accent which only the exceedingly posh can ever achieve.

'Oh – hello. I'd forgotten you were due to call', I said with a shrug. As if he'd believe that.

'Can we meet for a drink some time? Totally off the record, yah?' he asked.

'Well, let me check my diary … ' I rapidly flicked some random pieces of paper so it would sound like I was checking whether I had space in the diary that I had (as ever) forgotten to take off my desk at home. 'Well, actually', I explained, 'I have got a window in my schedule, err … NOW!' Okay, too desperate. Calm. Calm. 'I mean, if that's okay, it's just that the rest of this week is terribly … '

'Okay. Where?'

Three minutes of agonising small-talk and sipping Pepsi. Oh, god, I just want to ask you if he said yes. Enough already!

'So, err, did you get a chance to … '

'Look. I tried. I talked around the subject. I mentioned that I had seen your article … '

– I was virtually panting by this point. Morton megabucks, here I come –

' … and he hated it.'

I pasted a smile onto my face. 'I'm a hardened journo, me', it was meant to say. Burst into tears just because one person hated my article? Pah! I grinned as hard as I could.

'Do you want a tissue?' he said.

'That obvious? No, I'm fine. Why did he hate it?'

'His dad went mental. The Queen went mental. He was forced to have arguments he wanted to put off for a few years.'

'So I *was* right?'

He swigged from his glass of gin. 'Johann – of *course* you were.'

We talked for over two hours that day, and much of that conversation informs the chapter on William in this book. By the end of our long chat, my source was obviously getting anxious. He was slightly drunk and perhaps realised that the alcohol had loosened his tongue a little too much. He excused himself with a brisk handshake and strode off, a little too purposefully given the gin he'd been drinking all night, because he walked straight into a pillar.

This is how royal history gets made, I thought: by rat-arsed posh people walking into pillars. I tried ringing him lots of times in the next few months; I always got his answer-phone. He has never returned my calls.

So, alas, what you're holding isn't 'William: His True Story', or anything like it. But it *is* an informed insight into the very cruel world William has been forced into. What I am trying to craft here is a new argument about monarchy, and it is one I now know William agrees with. I support all the old republican principles, but, frankly, they aren't winning the argument yet. So we need a new, William-esque republicanism (apologies for sounding a bit Tony Blair circa 1997 here) which argues that not only is monarchy bad for Britain, it's bad for the Windsor family themselves.

As I ploughed through the research for this book, I was amazed again and again by how blindingly obvious it is that the monarchy has broken and destroyed each of the Windsor family in turn. We must not let this happen to William and Harry, and their children, and their children, and their children, and so on, verily until the Apocalypse. The monarchy is now an institution that can only produce psychologically and emotionally destroyed, unhappy people. It's time we ended the misery. This, then, is how the centuries of British monarchy will end: not with the bang of a revolution but with the whimper of a Prince.

But in order to get to the day when the Windsors are set free from the monarchy, it is necessary to do something which no doubt monarchist critics of this book will accuse of hypocrisy. We must intrude into the Windsors' privacy. We must draw on sources (including the tapes of private conversations which were, disgustingly, made public by the tabloids) which should not exist because they are so intrusive. Yet one of our central arguments against the monarchy is that it opens up the individuals at its heart to a completely unsustainable degree of monitoring and supervision by the media. So how can we justify doing the very thing we're attacking?

In order to show how intrusion has psychologically decimated the Windsors, we need to use the fruits of intrusion. All I can do is admit that I feel very uncomfortable doing it, and I hope in some small way it begins a debate which will end with the Windsor family being released from intrusion. I pledge – and I expect all decent republicans to do the same – that once the Windsor family retires from public life and ends the institution of monarchy (an event which I fully believe will happen within my lifetime), I will never write about them ever again, and I will violently condemn anyone who does. The intrusion into their privacy within this book is a regrettable necessity designed to show how the monarchy has damaged the Windsors. It is a means to an end: setting us on the road to the rescuing of the Windsor family from the clutches of the cruel institution which is destroying their lives.

Of course, there are some decent and honourable republicans who say it is wrong to talk about the Windsors at all. Tony Benn opposes the personalisation of this debate; it should, he argues, be about constitutional principles. Against this, I argue that in practice the British monarchy is inextricable from the Windsor family. Nobody seriously suggests that we could keep the institution of monarchy but ditch the Windsors. We'd have to find a new royal family – and though the House of Beckham would certainly be tempting, it's extremely unlikely.

We cannot discuss the monarchy, then, without discussing the individual Windsors. Prince Charles himself, in an interview in 2001, made it clear that personalities are central to any debate about monarchy. When Mary Riddell asked him what monarchy was about, he replied, 'God, all I can talk about is the way *I* think it should be. That is not necessarily how my successors see it. It is a personal thing, the whole business of monarchy.' Similarly, in the 1992 BBC documentary 'Elizabeth R', Elizabeth says, 'In this existence, the job and the life go together – you can't really divide it up.' So both Charles and Elizabeth have placed their own personalities at the absolute centre of the debate. If they are prepared to do that, I am only too happy to discuss it in their terms.

The monarchists have unashamedly used any favourable aspects of the personalities of the

Windsor family to bolster the institution; we republicans are therefore perfectly entitled to reciprocate by discussing those very personalities.

When he retired as Palace Press Spokesman in 1967, the famously reactionary Commander Colville publicly expressed his prescient fears about the lives of the Windsors being 'progressively more exposed to public scrutiny', and he said that there was difficulty distinguishing between 'what may be properly termed as "in the public interest" and what is private'. He seemed to think that a line could be drawn in the sand and consensus achieved about where this division lay. But he misunderstood the fact that monarchy in a celebrity age can only sell the individuals at its heart, and once it begins to sell that product, it cannot control the appetite for it. It cannot say, thus far and no more; it cannot reserve anything for the private individuals at its core.

The justification behind press intrusion into private lives of the famous is that the celebrities have asked for it – and monarchy cannot exist without asking for it. The royal family are therefore doomed to perpetual press intrusion against which they have very few sensible retorts, and certainly no effective ones. The days are gone when the Windsor family thrust themselves and their newborn babies into the public spotlight and expected nothing but praise in return.

This is not to attack the royals and say that therefore they *must* surrender their privacy. Rather, we need to all agree that nobody should be put in a position where they are forced to make that choice. It's nobody's fault that we ended up with this situation. Nobody planned to put people in this untenable position. It's just that, by chance, the monarchy has evolved over time in a way which makes it unbearably cruel to the individuals who happen to be the royal family.

You might be feeling sceptical about this argument right now. So: let's look at each of the Windsor family in turn ...

1

WILLIAM WINDSOR

The One Who Might Get Away

One man has the power to bring the monarchy to the brink of destruction. No, not our best republican journalist Jonathan Freedland, nor our best republican rabble-rouser Tony Benn, nor even our constitutional moderniser Tony Blair. The man who could finally herald the Republic of Britain is a nineteen-year-old named William Windsor – or, as the history books might record him, William the Last.

I was first alerted to the fact that Wills might not want to go into the family business when I read a suggestive quote made by his mother in an interview with Jennie Bond, the BBC's Royalty Correspondent. In an interview shortly before she died, Diana told Bond that William had comforted her by telling her she was 'very lucky to be able to give up the HRH'.

That, of course, was far from unambiguous. So I did a little more digging, and I was amazed by how much evidence from authoritative sources (unreported in the UK media, of course) proved that William really is a republican. Christopher Andersen, for example, is no *National Enquirer* hack; he is a contributing editor of *Time* magazine, the USA's organ of record. He revealed in his heavily researched book *Diana's Boys* that on more than one tearful occasion, William told his parents that he would never agree to become the monarch. He told Charles that he might 'go backpacking in Nepal and never come back'.

This wasn't just adolescent petulance. On his eighteenth birthday, William should have become His Royal Highness Prince William of Wales; he refused point-blank to accept the title. William has also refused to have a significant role in the Jubilee. His father has covered this up by pretending that he has instructed William not to disrupt his studies at St Andrews.

Nicholas Davies, the royal expert, has revealed

that during one holiday in his mid-teens, William was tobogganing down a steep hill in the dark. When he neared the bottom of the slope where cars were passing, a bodyguard leapt out, seemingly from nowhere. Seeing that William was hurtling towards speeding traffic, he threw himself onto the sledge and sent William hurtling into a pile of snow. William screamed, 'Why do I have to be surrounded by policemen all the time? Why won't you just let me be a normal person?'

It's a good question: why won't we let him be a normal person? We certainly could. Constitutionally, the throne could easily pass to William's younger brother Harry. But all the evidence suggests that Harry is even more wilful, individualistic and ill-inclined to sublimate all his energies into a pleasureless life of 'duty' than Wills. Of course, there would be a precedent in living memory for William's choice. The only voluntary abdication in history is that of Edward VIII in 1936. Yet William's inclinations demonstrate that if monarchy continues much longer, it will have to survive wave after wave of abdications. How many children in the twenty-first century will meekly accept that they will never have the chance to determine their own lives? Even if William is talked round to being King – a scenario which I think is seriously unlikely – will his children be happy to surrender their privacy and their lives? Will their children? Edward VIII described himself as 'wily enough to escape the web of an outmoded institution that has become no more than a government department'. Sooner or later, a whole string of would-be monarchs will feel the same way.

Indeed, if we look back at previous monarchs, many of them abdicated in all but name at some point in their lives. Following the death of her beloved Albert on 14 December 1861, Victoria retreated almost entirely from public life, refusing even to perform basic state duties like the opening of parliament. No contemporary monarch would be allowed to behave in this way without abdicating. Victoria chose to walk away from it all, even though she had the inducement of substantial and very real power. Future monarchs won't even have that to coax them to stay.

William's abdication could be lethal for the monarchy if he accompanied his resignation with a damning public statement making it clear that raising another child in the uniquely cruel goldfish bowl of British monarchy would be intolerable. If that seems unlikely, imagine the life we know William has been forced to lead. From the time he was a baby, he has had no privacy. Diana confided to Lord Deedes, a journalist, that, 'I'm worried that when William goes into the park with his nanny and needs to wee-wee, a photographer will jump out of the bushes and catch him on film.' It was a prescient fear, because only a few months later, exactly that sequence of events occurred. William has not even been able to take a piss in private.

Wherever he goes, he is followed by an armed private detective who is at most fifty yards behind. On his first day at school, there were 150 photographers waiting for him. His primary school had to have its windows replaced with bullet-proof glass. He has been threatened with anthrax attacks by terrorist groups. He had to be driven even from his school to its playing fields in his last year at Eton, in order to avoid the paparazzi.

William's moments of anonymity are so precious that he can list them. In 1999, he was representing his school in a cricket match. The scorer walked up to him in a tea break and brusquely demanded to know his name. He said simply, 'William.' The scorer snapped, 'William who?' When it was explained by the other boys who he was, the scorer was profusely apologetic, but William nearly cried as he said, 'Thank you. Thank you! You don't know what that just meant to me.'

William has seen the institution of monarchy destroy the lives of his parents. On holiday in St Tropez shortly before she died, Diana told reporters that, 'my boys are urging me to leave the country. They say it's the only way … William is stressed, William gets really freaked out.' Famously, William was the one to comfort Diana when she suffered at the hands of the press. He once pushed some tissues under the bathroom door and said, 'Don't cry, Mummy.' While holidaying with her in Lech, Austria, in

1995, William reacted with fury when a group of photographers broke an agreement that they would take no more photos of Diana that day. He had an aggressive altercation with them and threatened to take their cameras away. The situation was resolved only after a personal detective reasoned with him and secured a promise from the photographers that they would leave.

William firmly believes that the press killed his mother. His friend explained, 'He had been in situations with her before when they'd had to speed away from paparazzi. He had been scared [at that time]. So he could picture the scene [of her death] exactly ... He knew how terrifying it was. He is absolutely convinced that if it were not for the paparazzi, his mother would not have been speeding and she would be alive today. He calls them murderers, even now. I heard him say it a few weeks ago. He hates newspapers. He never reads them ... If he sees his photo in them, he looks away. He doesn't want to hear stories about himself; he just calls it all lies. He even told me once – a few years ago, mind – that I had blood on my hands because I buy the *Sun*. He will never, ever reconcile himself to the press. It's like in cartoons – they are his arch-enemy … You just can't imagine a time when he'll say, "oh, all right then". He will hate them until he dies.'

William very much shares, then, the view of his uncle, Charles Spencer, who said, 'it would appear that every proprietor and editor of every publication that has paid for intrusive, exploitative photographs of her, encouraging greedy and ruthless individuals to risk everything in pursuit of Diana's image, has blood on his hands.'

Evidence for his visceral hatred of the press litters his life story. He chose his university specifically because it was far away from the London media. He rides a motorbike in St Andrews because it makes it much harder to photograph him if he is travelling at speed. In 1997, he asked his parents not to come to his Sport's Day because the press attention would ruin it for everyone. Even in his eighteenth-birthday interview, when he was on his best behaviour, William stressed that he was 'uncomfortable' with the press attention. Diana said that, 'he hates the press even more than I did when I first got into this family. He sees them as the enemy.'

One event reveals succinctly his whole attitude. While William was on holiday in the South of France with his mother in 1996, they stayed in a villa which unfortunately could be seen from woods about 200 yards away. This was a public place from which photographers could spy on their every move. William became so determined not to give them anything at all that he refused to leave the villa during daylight hours. After several days of this, the holiday was cut short, and they returned to London.

Yet what is the monarchy now, if not a ceaseless media roadshow, selling nothing but itself? How can the royal family exist in the public consciousness, if not through the flashbulbs and omnipresent cameras? A prince who hates the press is a prince who cannot do his job. 'William knows that', his friend told me. 'That's why he wants to walk away from it now.'

And the removal of his privacy is not the only problem William has to endure unless he quits the monarchy. He has no freedom to choose a job, one of the key building blocks of identity for our generation. When William was ten, he said he'd like to be a policeman; Harry said, 'You can't be a policeman. You've got to be a King.' He was right. There is another key deprivation in William's life. Suppose, while at university, William experiments with different faiths. Suppose, like his mother, he begins to see the appeal of Islam, or Scientology, or Sikhism, or – heaven forbid! – atheism. What then? He was born to be head of the Church of England. So we rob him of one of the most basic human rights: religious freedom.

That isn't enough though. We've taken his privacy and his beliefs, but we want another pound of flesh too. There are whole Websites dedicated to the belief that William is gay. This is untrue, and the sensible sites admit that they have no more evidence than the prettiness of his eyelashes. But what if William had been gay? Could he have had a gay partner as royal consort?

You can imagine the *Sun* headline: 'Two Queens at the Palace'. These issues will crop up with a monarch sooner or later, if the institution isn't abolished.

A straight William will not be much better off. According to the reputable end of the American press, several government agencies monitor any girls in which William expresses a romantic interest, 'for security purposes'. One paper quoted 'a former member of parliament with close links to the palace', who said that, after all the scandalous headlines, 'the Queen pays very close attention to the girls in William's life to avoid another Diana or Fergie'. Can you think of anything more hideous for a young lad than for his granny to be vetting his shags?

If William experimented with drugs, like his brother Harry, cousin Frederick or pretty much anyone else of his age, he would find his photo splashed across the front pages. Frederick explained, after he was revealed to have used coke, that, 'it is very hard to avoid getting into this sort of thing if you move in these circles'. That is as true of William as it was of his cousin, although his friend told me that, as far as he knows, William has avoided drugs other than alcohol and tobacco.

William is forced to surrender his privacy, his sexual freedom, his religious freedom, his chemical freedom, his political freedom (he is not even allowed to vote, never mind speak out on political affairs), and for what? For the glory of one day being King? A glory that consists of, um, unveiling statues and blundering around in carriages, waving like a buffoon to an increasingly resentful and chippy public? Would you do it? 'Let's face it', his friend told me, 'it's not exactly the most tempting gig in the world, is it?'

And William has a greater ability to walk away from the monarchy than any other heir to the throne in history. William has an immense personal fortune completely unconnected to his royal status – a unique situation. No matter how rich Charles Windsor appears to be, if he gave up his connections to 'the Firm', there would be a huge conflict over whether he owned any of it at all. The Duchy of Cornwall, the source of virtually all his income, is owned not by Charles but by whoever happens to be Prince of Wales. If he surrenders the title, he surrenders the wealth. Edward VIII was dependent entirely on his brother's generosity after he abdicated, and had almost no personal funds at all. William, in contrast, is sitting on a cool £8 million in the bank, inherited from his mother. She achieved this one final blow towards the Windsor family, even in death.

William could, therefore, live a private life of luxury far from the draughty palaces of Britain. Indeed, all his life choices so far indicate that he wants to live the carefree decadent aristocratic lifestyle of his friends. He wanted to spend his gap year playing polo in Argentina. Instead, he was forced by his father (and a committee including former Cabinet Minister Chris Patten and George Carey, the Archbishop of Canterbury, convened to 'discuss' his gap year) to choose a more media-friendly project.

Elizabeth Windsor was always told by her mother that her 'duties' (the sacrifice of a meaningful, self-determined life) were 'the rent you pay for the room you occupy on earth'. If

Charles tried to tell William that, I hope he laughed. It is the language of another age. William has learned far more from his mother, who in many ways epitomises the spirit of individualism tempered with sympathy for others. It is a very different brew to the old, passive notion of duty.

We live in far too individualistic an age for us to expect one boy, randomly plucked, to sublimate his entire life to the arid concept of 'duty'. In the 1950s, it was possible: after all, a whole generation of men were heroically being called upon to sacrifice their lives to combat fascism, and a whole generation of women were similarly being called upon to accept massive deprivations for the same reason. So there was a bridging period after the monarchy lost most of its power, in which the individuals at its head could be induced to sacrifice themselves because *everyone* was being sacrificed, one way or another. Elizabeth Windsor was a product of that time, as we can see when she said (in the documentary 'Elizabeth R'), 'It's just a question of maturing into what you're doing and accepting that here you are and that's your fate.' The generation that could yield such stoical, self-sacrificing monarchs is passing into history.

It was in autumn 2000 that William first had a sustained, adult conversation (rather than a row) with his father, in which he made it clear that he had given it considerable thought and he really, really didn't want to be King. His father remains convinced that this is just a teenage phase – but he is now nineteen and has been resolved within his own mind on this issue for four years. How long can a phase last before it becomes a settled, immutable belief? Charles has tried to get other people to intervene to persuade William that he must be monarch. Mark Dyer was William's guard during his gap year, and he was asked to talk William round. They had many long conversations, but William was unwavering and clear: he will never be King.

Indeed, it was reported by journalists close to Charles that he was concerned about William's 'headstrong' nature as long ago as 1998. William arranged ski trips where he travelled as a 'normal' passenger. He refused to play by the rules of normal royal protocol, finding them ridiculous, and began to smart at the round-the-clock surveillance he is put under by the security services.

The psychological pressure the monarchy has heaped upon William is immense. In July 1996, when William was *fourteen,* he was put on the cover of *Time* magazine with the oppressive headline, 'Can This Boy Save the Monarchy?' The monarchy has also put severe strains on William's relations with his relatives. As his close friend explained, 'William doesn't like the Queen. He likes Philip, who he thinks has some spirit like his mum, although they've had quite a few rows in their time. But he thinks the Queen is cold ... He can never relax when she's around because everyone there is obsessed with protocol and all that stuff his mum taught him to hate ... He has to bow to her, which he thinks is silly .... Diana always showed respect for the Queen around William, even when she was really upset, but William sensed that [Elizabeth] treated his mum badly. William is polite to her because his dad would be very upset if he wasn't.'

There was a turning point in his relationship with his paternal grandmother: 'The Queen made a mistake when she messed William around in the week after Diana died. He really wanted to go to London to thank everyone for all the flowers and cards, but the Queen said no for days and days. She let Andrew and Edward go and do a walkabout, and she gave a speech [on TV] herself, before William and Harry were eventually allowed to [go to the Palace and greet the crowds]. He has never forgiven her for that.' Elizabeth Windsor seemed to feel that William and Harry's presence would bolster the pro-Diana mood in London and further damage the wider Windsor dynasty. 'He feels she put the good of the monarchy before the good of her own grandchildren. It's a whole mindset William hates ... The Queen's displeasure, which is something all the other royals fear, doesn't worry William. He knows his dad will be devastated when he doesn't take the throne and that worries him, but the Queen? No. That's not a worry for him really.'

Charles Spencer said at Diana's funeral – in a

clear attack on Elizabeth Windsor – that he would continue 'the imaginative and loving way in which you [Diana] were steering these two exceptional young men, so that their souls are not simply immersed by duty and tradition but can sing openly as you planned'. William very much took this to heart. He promised himself that he would never allow his soul to be immersed by duty and tradition – and that meant ditching the institution, monarchy, which had killed one parent and broken another.

What will ultimately destroy the monarchy, then, is not republicanism (though that will help). No, it will be the sheer inhumanity of monarchy in a celebrity-obsessed, twenty-four-hour media culture. Prince William, conscious of the terrible effect this had on his mother, will walk away before the press can argue that, like Diana, he's 'asking for it', 'thrusting himself into the limelight' or 'loving the attention'. As it stands, he can make an unimpeachable case that he deserves to be left alone.

In time, he would fade into the obscurity enjoyed by other celebrities' children. Who, for example, knows where Tricia Nixon is now? Yet during her father's presidency, her face was recognised all over the world. The clock is ticking on that option for William though – and he knows it. 'When he leaves Uni', his friend explained to me, 'and that might be sooner than you think because he doesn't like it there ... he's going to have to go public. He knows that. He's going to make it perfectly clear that he won't let the monarchy ruin *his* life.'

2

ELIZABETH

A Character Study of How Monarchy Can Wreck Your Life

When we celebrate fifty years of Elizabeth's 'reign', we are in truth celebrating fifty years of misery and deprivation imposed on one poor, desperate woman. No. Actually, it is over seven decades of abuse, for Elizabeth Windsor has *never* known normality. The life of Elizabeth serves as an instructive lesson to William. She has served a sentence he is resolved to avoid at all costs.

It is hard to know where to begin when tabulating the damage the monarchy has done to Elizabeth. Perhaps it is best to start by looking at the one, brief period of her life in which she was able to escape its clutches. When she first married Philip Mountbatten, she travelled to Malta where she lived from 1950 to 1951 as a comparatively normal Navy-man's wife. Marian Crawford – who, as Elizabeth's nanny, was to all intents and purposes Elizabeth's mother, as we understand the role today – explained very clearly the impact that this time in Malta had on Elizabeth. 'The Princess had no very clear understanding of the way people lived outside Palace walls. But when she flew to visit Prince Philip in Malta, she saw and experienced for the first time the life of an ordinary girl not living in a Palace.'

This period is invariably described by Elizabeth's friends as her happiest time. She was allowed to be a normal aristocratic woman, socialising, having tea and generally being an officer's wife around town. She could see for the only time the life that she might have had if only the monarchy had not existed. She was in Paradise. A very good friend of Elizabeth's, Lady Kennard, has said that, 'I'm quite sure that the first five years they spent together [before Elizabeth became Queen] were the happiest days of their life. The Princess [as she then was] was able to live just like an ordinary naval officer's wife and it was the only time that she lived such a free life.'

Her closest friend, Patricia Mountbatten, has explained that being wrenched from this life was 'a tragedy ... From the Queen's point of view it was a disaster that it all [i.e. becoming monarch] happened so soon'. Or, we could add, that it happened at all. It is the monarchists and their demands who wrenched her from this dream-world.

Either side of this period of bliss, there is a life of such uncompromising weirdness that we have to look to Michael Jackson, paraded from birth as a performing freak, to find another child who was so ruthlessly pressed into the public eye from infancy. Elizabeth's childhood is invariably presented in monarchist propaganda as a time of unbroken happiness. This is in blatant contradiction of the facts.

True, there is one other moment of freedom from the monarchy on record. On VE Day in 1945, Elizabeth walked through the crowds wearing a cap pulled down over her eyes. She joined in the hysteria, doing the Lambeth Walk and the hokey-cokey. This was a precious moment of ordinary life which was never to be repeated, although Elizabeth has often described it to friends as the most exhilarating of her life. Her children and grandchildren, whose faces were known to everyone from the moment of birth, were to be staved of even these precious seconds.

For Elizabeth, all else has been strangeness and misery. As a child, Elizabeth witnessed the institution of monarchy reduce her father to a gibbering wreck. The poor man hated appearing in public, and suffered from a severe stammer. He hated speaking so much that many people believed he was retarded. When his brother abdicated and it became clear that he would have to be King, Elizabeth's father became nearly hysterical. He described it as 'a dreadful moment', and he feared he wouldn't be able to get through his Coronation vows without an attack of stammering and possibly even a breakdown. He told his friend Ramsay MacDonald that he was so sickened during the ceremony that he was entirely unaware of what was happening. What can witnessing all of this have made the young Elizabeth feel about the fate that awaited her? Is it any wonder that, as Lord Strathmore said, the young girl, when she realised that she too would have to suffer in this way, began to 'pray for a brother' who would take precedence over her in the succession and save her from becoming monarch?

Elizabeth from babyhood was subject to relentless public analysis. Immediately after giving birth, her mother began to market her child for her own selfish purposes. She authorised a biography of her baby, without any concern for how infringing the child's privacy might impact upon her later in life. After the war, her mother stepped up the shameless exploitation of her daughter by appointing the first royal press officer to sell details of her private life to the British public.

Elizabeth was just three years old when she first made the cover of *Time* magazine. Even Elizabeth Bowes-Lyon sensed that the hysteria surrounding her daughter was dangerous. She wrote to Queen Mary that, 'It almost frightens me that people love her so much.' At the age of ten, she was described (at a time when most kids want to run around their home jumping on beds and having pillow fights) as possessing 'great charm and a natural unassumptive dignity'. Did anybody ask what the effect of ascribing such unnatural adult qualities to a child would be? Did anyone care? Elizabeth was strictly instructed not to allow herself to behave like a normal child. Her friend Lady Mountbatten explains that, 'she was very aware that how she behaved in public was very important. For instance … she knew she must try not to cry.' This had devastating effects on the formation of her personality.

The Queen and her sister were raised in a gilded cage and very rarely glimpsed the real world. As her nanny and de facto mother Marian Crawford said, 'In those days we lived in an ivory tower removed from the real world.' Her descriptions of a little girl who would stand staring out of the window and ask about 'the world outside' are almost unbearable because they depict a neglected and ill-treated child. She told a man who came to paint her portrait that she would stare at the people who passed and 'wonder what they were doing and where they were all going, and what they thought about outside the Palace'.

Sealed off from the normal social interaction of school, Elizabeth found it hard to make friends. Crawford describes a 'rather special friendship' that she fleetingly formed with the daughter of a neighbour, but this ended when the friend was sent away to school and Elizabeth was left, once more, alone. She has never at any point been able to have a proper friend. One ex-lady-in-waiting told Ben Pimlott that the royals 'never have entirely normal relationships. Even your best friends like Porchey ['Lord' Porchester], or oldest courtiers like Martin Charteris, treat you with special courtesy.' Patricia Mountbatten, Elizabeth's best friend, has said, 'I never for a moment forget that she is my sovereign.' What a great friendship *that* must be – and yet it is Elizabeth's closest.

Every tiny ailment Elizabeth suffered found its way into the press. She must have been constantly aware of being watched. Yet her parents simply told her that this was her fate and that she had no choice but to accept it. The extent to which Elizabeth Windsor's life has been pushed by monarchy into the public domain is astonishing. For example, we know definitively (because semi-authorised royal author Brian Hoey discloses it) that each morning Elizabeth takes a bath which is exactly 62 degrees centigrade (her maid tests it with a thermometer), and it is never more than seven inches deep. She prefers to bathe in 'a deep, old-fashioned Victorian cast-iron bath with massive brass taps', and so on and so on.

'Duty' was so vehemently drummed into her by her parents that, as Philip Mountbatten once said, 'If it was customary to have porridge at every meal, Lillibet [Elizabeth] would have it.' Elizabeth has been forced to submit her life for public consumption because she was told that it was her 'duty' and that she would be betraying her family, her country and God if she refused it. For these reasons she was forced into public work from adolescence. She delivered her first broadcast at the age of fourteen, and inspected her first regiment at sixteen.

As if to compound the misery that this uniquely awful childhood brought, Elizabeth was subjected to systematic and deliberate parental neglect. As with so many victims of poor parenting, she in turn inflicted her experience on her own children. The 'requirements of royalty' meant that her parents abandoned their small children for months on end, entrusting them to anonymous nannies. They jetted off to Australia for six months when their child couldn't even talk, and barely recognised her when they returned. If a working-class woman living on a council estate behaved in this way, she would be slammed as 'the worst mother in Britain', a 'home-alone mum', 'unfit to raise kids', and so on. With shocking dishonesty, when Elizabeth Bowes-Lyon was asked what her main duty was, she said it was 'to bring up my children'.

Elizabeth was to continue this tragic cycle and show similar breathtaking cruelty to her own kids. When her son was just three years old, she abandoned him for six months to travel abroad. She had so little feeling for her own baby that even when she returned to England, she spent four days dealing with paperwork and another day at the races before at last she deigned to see the desperate child. When finally they were reunited, the tiny boy was forced to wait in line to *shake his mother's hand.* This chilling lack of maternal feeling (which considerably exceeds the cultural pressures on an upper-class woman of the time not to show excessive emotion) has yet to be absorbed by the British public. In 1977, the Queen could still accept plaudits from writers like John Grigg who said that, 'she has shown how much family life means to her, and she has stood rock-firm for all she represents'.

Even now, her relationship with her children shows an inhuman formality. Even though they often stay in the same building as her, her kids can't simply pop their head round the door for a chat. If ever they wish to see her, they must despatch a page, who will make an appointment for them. When they are discussing her with 'an outsider' (a non-royal), they refer to their parents as 'Her Majesty' or 'His Royal Highness'. They bow their heads when they greet their parents and would never dream of wearing casual clothes in their presence. Douglas Hurd has described it well; he says that Elizabeth's 'constitutional machinery' is in tip-top shape, but her 'emotional machinery' is almost entirely out of order.

Brian Hoey's biography of Elizabeth has a telling, tiny detail about Elizabeth's relationship with her daughter which speaks volumes. He was chatting with Anne Windsor, when her mother called. Anne instinctively stood to attention as she spoke to Elizabeth on the telephone. He explains that, 'it appeared to be an unconscious act resulting from an upbringing which instilled good manners ... when addressing the sovereign, and it was somehow symbolic of the attitudes within the royal family that divide them from the rest of us'. Can you imagine a mother who instils this kind of behaviour in her babies?

Michael Mann, the former Dean of Windsor, has revealed that Elizabeth is still at times neglectful and cruel to her children: 'When Princess Anne and Tim Laurence came to me to talk about getting married, I asked her: "Have you spoken to your mother?" Anne replied: "You know how difficult it is to talk to Mummy about these things. Aunty Margaret always says that the only time to see her is when she's on her own and the dogs are not there – and then she is usually too tired." It took Anne three weeks before she could nail her mother to a date.'

It is *absolutely crucial* to understand that Elizabeth Windsor is *not* like this because she is just that kind of person; she has become this way *directly because of the impact of the monarchy*. Don't take my word for it. Just listen to the words of her closest friend, Patricia Mountbatten: 'You see, *if you are brought up to live your life in the eyes of the world*, you can't afford to be seen to be terribly sad, or in tears or cross or even unwell. You have to have such total control over yourself at all times that it then becomes quite difficult to show your emotions, even in private. *I think that is a particular thing with the royal family* – they cannot be seen to be other than totally composed and in control of the situation in public, and that spills over into their private life.' [My italics]

The thesis of this book could not be stated more succinctly than it is here by a person who has observed the monarchy at closer quarters than *almost* anyone else alive. Elizabeth Windsor's deep character flaws (which have most obviously manifested themselves in the cruel neglect of her children) are directly attributable to the institution of monarchy. It has deformed her character so that she cannot have a functioning private life.

This has been confirmed again and again by those who know her best. Lord Charteris, her former private secretary (a man who spent every working day with her for over a decade), said that the key to the Queen's character is that she is 'afraid of her emotions'. This is, he confirms, a product of her job. One of her most senior ladies-in-waiting told *Telegraph* journalist Graham Turner, 'the Queen does not like emotion, and for very good reasons'. She went on to explain that if you showed your emotions, this might spill over into your constitutional role. So, as former Foreign Secretary Douglas Hurd, who accompanied Elizabeth on many state visits, explains, for her job '*she has almost trained feelings out of herself*' [My italics]. A friend of Elizabeth's told Nigel Dempster that, 'even when she tells you what she thinks, you never know what she feels'. Who can doubt now that this is an inhuman and cruel job which should go the way of child chimney sweeps and be abolished for the mental health of those involved?

The institution of monarchy directly turned Elizabeth into a bad mother. As Anthony Jay, who scripted the documentary 'Elizabeth R', explains, 'She's one of those people who is deeply unemotional ... For people who are emotionally detached in that way, institutions become more important than families. The Queen's children were handed over to nannies, and a kind of emotional cauterisation took place. Something was sealed off very early. For her, that is a strength. *If she were emotionally involved, she couldn't do her job.*' [My italics]

Elizabeth can have normal relations with neither her children nor her friends. She has always been so surrounded by sycophants that she has to turn to animals, especially dogs and horses, for non-deferential treatment. Sir John Miller, who was the Crown Equerry in charge of the Royal Mews, says that, 'Her Majesty prefers animals to human beings. For one thing, they don't talk so much.' Bill Meldrum, who has been a gamekeeper at Sandringham for many years, explains why: 'To a dog, it doesn't matter whether you're the Queen or a down-and-out living on the streets of London. The Queen's dogs love her and nobody else; but not because she's the Queen. There are a lot of people around her who say things they think she wants to hear, but from her dogs, she gets total honesty.'

A tragic picture emerges from these descriptions, of a woman who has never known, and will never know, normal social interaction and can at best derive 'truth' from her dogs. The monarchists are proud to have broken poor Elizabeth Windsor in this way: they call it 'duty'. Her job – a job no human being should be forced to do – demands that she become isolated in this way. As one former courtier told *Telegraph* journalist Graham Turner, 'the day you're natural with the Queen is the end of the monarchy. If you were not to get butterflies in your stomach when you met her, she would just be an ordinary person. But how awful it must be when nobody can be themselves with you.'

As with so many victims of abuse, Elizabeth has internalised the dictates of her abusers. She now will not allow anybody to behave normally around her: it seems to make her feel uncomfortable. For example, Admiral Robert Woodard, who was in charge of the Royal Yacht *Britannia* for five years, has said that, 'it is very easy to fall into the error of over-familiarity. You then realise that you are beginning to treat her as *a normal person,* and *that can't be allowed.* When I went over the top, her eyebrows would go up and I'd apologise. She hoped you would sort out the *distance you needed to keep.*' [My italics]

Elizabeth's obsession with a cold formality at the expense of normal human warmth is, then, obvious – and it extends even to her close relatives. Sarah Ferguson has recalled one example of this. The Windsor family were holidaying at Balmoral, and Andrew and Sarah were staying after the others left. When Elizabeth's car departed, the family were lined up for a formal farewell in which they all stood in order of rank (*to bid farewell to their mum and dad* – how weird is that?). Fergie walked along as the car was leaving and shouted 'Bye-bye!' at the top of her voice; Elizabeth, disgusted, 'looked daggers'. For perfectly normal, *human* behaviour like this, Sarah was damned as 'vulgar, vulgar, vulgar'.

A small taste of how Elizabeth experiences the world, in a strange way entirely unlike anybody else, can be found in the sycophantic film *The Royal Family*, made in 1969. Even a man as experienced in meeting the famous and powerful as the American Ambassador begins to panic when he sees her. He is so frightened and awed that when she asks if he is living in the Embassy at the moment, he stammers, 'we are in the embassy residence, subject of course to some discomfiture as a result of a need for elements of refurbishing, rehabilitation'. If this is the gibberish that an experienced diplomat talks to the Queen, can you imagine the nonsense that everyone else speaks to her? What picture can she possibly have gained of the world, given that everyone who interacts with her sees her not as a normal woman but as The Queen? Even her favourite private secretary and friend, Lord Charteris, has said that he never forgot her royal status 'for a second'. How can we expect this woman, who has never had a normal conversation with a normal person ever – not a single time – to be normal and representative? The expectation is preposterous.

Not only have Elizabeth's relationships with her children and her friends been scuppered by the monarchy, her marriage has also been wrecked. She was never given the opportunity to select from a number of eligible men. Some argue that Elizabeth fell in love with Philip at an early age, but other insiders believe that she merely reconciled herself to 'what had to be'. As one person explained to Pimlott, 'there really was nobody she could possibly marry but Prince Philip'. After she was publicly associated with Philip Mountbatten, crowds would shout at her, 'Where's Philip?' whenever she was seen without him. She confided to her nanny Marian

Crawford that she found this process 'horrible'. Margaret Windsor put it well when she said to her sister, 'Poor Lillibet. *Nothing of your own. Not even your love affair.*' [My italics]

So, required to marry early and, in practice, to marry Philip Mountbatten, she was denied the ability to experiment romantically or sexually. This seems especially tragic since she is a woman who very much enjoys sex. Philip lamented to friends early in their marriage that Elizabeth was 'quite insatiable' and 'wouldn't let me out of bed'. She was also denied the vital ability to divorce. If she became unhappy with her marriage, tough. She couldn't separate without precipitating a constitutional crisis, something she would find intolerable because of the aggressive indoctrination she suffered as she grew up.

So, it is legitimate to ask: if Elizabeth Windsor had been a normal person, might she have wished to divorce? Has she been trapped in a relationship that a normal person would be free to escape?

Outside the UK, rumours of affairs and problems in the marriage have swept the international press, and it is a sign of how ludicrously quiescent the British press still is that these have never been clearly stated in print in Britain. One person who is very widely believed to be Philip's son is Max Boisot. Philip paid to send the lad to the school he insisted on for his other sons, Gordonstoun, although the boy's mother claims that this was simply an 'act of friendship' on Philip's part. It would certainly be a very generous act of friendship in a man otherwise noted for his stinginess. Even the ultra-monarchist Barbara Cartland admitted in interviews with Kitty Kelley that Philip had sired 'illegitimate' off-spring: 'I know all about Philip's illegitimate daughter in Melbourne', she said, 'but I'm not going to talk about it.'

Kelley extensively documents the sordid details of Philip's personal life. To cite but one example, well-respected royal author Brian Hoey told her on good authority that on the Prince's fantastically expensive 1956 'tour', 'a couple of lady typists were flown in to join the boat in Singapore. They didn't do much typing – they weren't the type.' Philip's friend Taki, the

Spectator columnist, has also been strikingly frank about Philip's personal life: 'Everyone knows that Sasha [the Duchess of Abercorn] is Philip's mistress ... she's lasted the longest, six to eight years.' Another person in the know who has discussed Philip's much-rumoured adultery is the late John Barrett, who had been Lord Mountbatten's private secretary. He said that Philip and Princess Alexandra 'have been long involved'.

Kelley tracked down a woman who was able to describe first-hand the sexually predatory behaviour of Philip. Regine Traulsen was an attractive Moroccan woman who entered Philip's social circle via the painter Felix Topolski, who has painted Philip and become friendly with him. She explained in passing that she thought the Prince was a very attractive man (and he was, physically at least). A few weeks later, Topolski told her that he had made an appointment for them to have sex in one of Philip's flats while the Queen was busy with the regatta. She declined, explaining that she wasn't interested in a one-night stand. 'I'm sure', she told Kelley, 'that I wasn't the only woman propositioned in this way.'

There has been much speculation that Philip's current mistress is Penny Romsey, the forty-eight-year-old who is wife to 'Lord' Romsey. Occasionally, the press hint at their affair. *Daily Mail* diarist Ephraim Hardcastle makes much play on their 'passion for carriage-driving' together. Philip doesn't even try to disguise their physical intimacy in public. At the Royal Yacht Squadron Ball last year, he ran his hands up and down her back, whispered softly into her ear, and generally behaved for all the world to see as if they were lovers. When a close family member, Timothy Knatchbull, got married, Philip was the only member of the family who didn't bother to show – he was having a weekend break with Penny Romsey. She has been pictured with her arms wrapped tightly around Philip as they jaunt on his motorbike, and in public they are, in the words of one onlooker, 'all over each other'. Their intimacy was revealed in 1996 in a secretly-taped phone conversation in which it became clear that they are emotionally very close indeed: one could almost say as close as a man and his wife.

Philip denies the affairs bluntly by saying, 'I have never moved anywhere without a policeman accompanying me. So how the hell could I get away with anything like that?' Yet royal police officers turned a blind eye to his grandson Harry's illegal under-age drinking and cannabis smoking – why on earth would they not turn a blind eye to Philip's over-age lovemaking? Indeed, Charles, Diana and Fergie all had policemen accompanying them just as much as Philip, and they managed to maintain a healthy programme of extra-marital activities.

We do not know Elizabeth's reaction to these rumours. It is perfectly possible that they have some kind of Clinton-esque agreement – spoken or unspoken – that she is prepared to ignore his women friends in return for all the other things he brings to her life. Waywardness in marriage is commonplace and not necessarily wrong. What is wrong is to put a woman in a position where she cannot escape from a husband who is adulterous. If her husband were adulterous and she disapproved,

Elizabeth Windsor would be trapped in a cruel situation where she could not divorce if she wanted to. Robert Lacey, a biographer of the Queen, says astutely that, 'It seems impossible that Elizabeth should not have felt the deepest hurt and betrayal at the moment she discovered the existence of someone else into whose eyes he stared.' Indeed, Elizabeth has paid a powerful snub to Philip by refusing to make him her official consort, as Victoria did with her beloved Albert. This might be a punishment for his philandering.

These matters aside, her marriage has been put under even further strain by the monarchy. Philip desperately wanted his children to take his surname, Mountbatten. The Churchill Government told her strictly that this was impossible, so Elizabeth publicly announced that her children would take the surname Windsor. Lord Mountbatten revealed that, 'Philip retaliated by moving out of her bed.' A normal couple freed from the monarchy would never have had to confront these strains.

A.N. Wilson has written with great insight about the marriage of Elizabeth and Philip. As he says, 'it is no secret that the Queen and her husband lead separate lives, and have done so for years ... it is a partnership based on much separation, and it is not what a bourgeois person would recognise as a "happy" marriage.' This is of course true, and it is extraordinary that what passes for a truism in royal circles is still not repeated in the public press. It seems fair to surmise, then, that it is possible that, if Elizabeth had been released from the prison of monarchy, she would have considered leaving Philip (if, indeed, she would ever have married him at all). As monarch, she is effectively forbidden to do so. Is this an illegitimate breach of basic human rights?

Of course there are some compensations for these abuses. The spin that Elizabeth is just a plain rural lady with no taste for extravagance is simply a lie. She lives in extraordinary luxury. This is a woman whose dogs have their own palatial suite next to her 'Page's Pantry'. Her corgis each have their own pure-silver bowl to drink from. Any milk she or her dogs allow to pass their lips has been produced fresh that day at her own private dairy in Windsor. Her rooms are stuffed full of fresh flowers by her own personal florist every morning. Her chauffeur is always waiting in case she wants to go anywhere. There are liveried footmen (note: foot*men* plural) at her beck and call, twenty-four-seven. She didn't enter a kitchen herself until she was in her twenties. Even her butter is carefully stamped with the royal cipher, as she wishes.

Elizabeth gives harsh orders to her staff. They are forced to bend to her every whim. She dislikes beards and moustaches, so everybody who works in any royal palace must shave daily. She dislikes men wearing waistcoats, so everybody in her employ is forbidden to wear one, ever.

Some would argue that her job is some compensation. While it is true that she enjoys considerable real powers (discussed in Part II), Neil Kinnock – who as Leader of the Opposition for over a decade saw Elizabeth's work closely – gives us a sense of how mind-numbingly boring her job is most of the time. He observed recently that, 'the great skill the Queen has acquired over the years is to use the word "fascinating" in about five different tones ... What she's developed over the years is the technique of giving evidence of really rapt interest and attention whilst at the same time being able to slip her mind into neutral.'

Despite the pain and deep unhappiness we as a nation have inflicted upon Elizabeth, still the monarchists say that we should continue to make her suffer. Indeed, we should be proud that we have done it, and, in turn, respect her for surrendering her life. *Respect* her? No. We should pity her, for we have destroyed her life. When I look at Elizabeth Windsor, I don't feel pride; I feel shame.

3

DIANA

A Character Study of How the Monarchy Can Wreck Your Sanity

Whatever happens in the twenty-first century, the image of Diana will hang over the monarchy forever. She provided my generation with our JFK moment, and for that alone we will never forget her. She is a strangely ambiguous icon though, as the reams of contradictory academic literature about her life already demonstrate. Yet her significance for the monarchy is comparatively clear.

Diana's terrible life provides proof positive that, as her friend Clive James told me in an interview, 'Monarchy is not compatible with a twenty-four-seven celebrity culture.' Diana's bad luck was to marry into the Windsor family at the moment when capitalist profit motives finally hollowed out any feudal sentiments of deference towards royal feelings. When Charles was a child studying at Cheam, a phone call from Commander Colville, then Palace Press Officer, was enough to stop intrusion into the child's life. By the time Diana arrived on the scene, that kind of Palace–press relationship was rotting in a grave dug by market forces.

A hugely significant symbolic moment occurred shortly after Charles and Diana's wedding. Diana was finding it impossible to cope with press attention which intruded into every second of her life. Elizabeth Windsor summoned Fleet Street editors to the Palace to lecture them on why this had to stop. In an earlier age, this would have scared them off. But in a properly capitalist society, the wishes of one little old lady, no matter how supposedly exalted, couldn't outweigh the instinct for profit. The *News of the World* editor, Barry Askew, asked why, if the Princess wanted privacy, she didn't send servants to do some of her shopping. Elizabeth, astonished that she was not commanding the respect she expected, snapped back, 'That was a pompous remark, Mr Askew.' This was the moment that the last vestige of British feudalism died. The Palace would never again be so naïve as to expect the old deference from people whose sole interest was to make hard cash.

That lack of deference – so good in some ways – also led to an intrusion into Diana's life which was literally intolerable. She barely spoke in public (she was once called the last great silent actress), so her appeal was forced to be visual: every inch of her body – from her hymen to her hair – was examined by sweaty male newspaper writers (and, perhaps even more despicably, by her 'sister' journalists too). This ceaseless analysis of her looks induced bulimia.

Inspected in a way she would never have been as a non-royal, Diana was found to be 'fat'. Leading British journalist Jean Rook wrote at the time of her wedding that Diana 'must learn to watch ... the ounce or two of puppy fat'. Other journalists euphemistically discussed her 'curvaceous figure'. Suddenly confronted with cutting demands that she must be physically perfect, Diana responded the only way she knew how: an eating disorder.

There is an agreement amongst her biographers that Diana only became bulimic after the royal glare was turned on her. Her former flatmate Caroline Bartholomew, who knew Diana as well as anyone, believes it is the pressure of monarchy that brought it on. 'She went to live at Buckingham Palace', she explained, 'and then the tears started. The little thing got so thin ... She wasn't happy, she was suddenly plunged into all this pressure and it was a nightmare for her.' Every time Diana rammed her fingers down the back of her throat, it was proof that the institution of monarchy was destroying another life.

But it wasn't only the scrutiny that the monarchy forced on Diana. It also imposed the improbable marriage she fell into. Diana knew herself before it even began that it wasn't going to work. She began to panic when she realised that her fiancée was clearly in love with another woman. Again, monarchy claimed its pound of flesh. Her sister Sarah said it plainly: 'It's bad luck, Duch. Your face is on the tea towels so it's too late to chicken out now.'

Charles felt incredibly pressured by the nature of monarchy to marry – and produce an heir. He dithered because, he explained, 'divorce is out of the question for someone like me. Therefore, one's decision must be that much more careful.' When the poor lad was only twenty, he stammered to an interviewer that marriage for him 'is awfully difficult, because you've got to remember that when you marry, in my position, you are going to marry somebody who perhaps one day is going to become queen. You've got to choose somebody very carefully ... People expect quite a lot from somebody like that ... and it has got to be someone pretty special.'

So Charles was never allowed to choose a woman who might suit him. As Steven Barry, his former valet and friend, explains, 'the women the Prince liked best ... were the ones who had experienced most'. Yet the monarchy demanded, in accordance with its bizarre tradition, that he choose the exact opposite of the women he liked: a virgin. (Lord Fermoy, Diana's uncle, said publicly that, 'Diana, I can assure you, has never had a lover ... Diana has never been involved with anybody in this way. This is good.' Before she even married into monarchy, chunks of her privacy were falling away.) Lord Mountbatten told Charles that falling in love was a luxury which a future King could not afford. (It is a curious fact that the most ardent pro-monarchists, like that shameless old sycophant Mountbatten, are also the most cruel and callous about the individuals at its core.)

Speculation about Charles's possible brides became ludicrous. The *Daily Express* splashed on its front page, 'CHARLES TO MARRY ASTRID – OFFICIAL'. This was a reference to 'Princess' Astrid 'of Belgium', who he had met once, briefly, several years before. He dictated an understandably tetchy press release which read: 'They are not getting engaged this Monday, next Monday or the Monday after, or any other Monday, Tuesday, Wednesday or Thursday. They do not know each other, and people who do not know each other do not get engaged.'

Many women who Charles liked very much were ruled out for reasons entirely beyond his control. Anna Wallace, his last great love affair before Diana appeared in the public eye, was disclosed – dun dun duuuunnnn – to have *had sex* with *more than one man!* Once the nation had absorbed this rampant harlotry (Princess Anne referred to the poor woman's previous lovers as 'the Wallace Collection'), they judged that this 'slut' was plainly not worthy to be Queen. Charles had to ditch her – the People demanded it. He abandoned all hope of marrying her, but couldn't bring himself to break it off. Eventually, Anna just walked away.

Because Charles waited what was considered a long time for a suitable woman (of course, he should have been entitled even to not marry, if he wanted to), there was a great deal of impatience when the apparently perfect Diana Spencer appeared. Charles was robbed of the freedom to choose his own wife (or choose to remain single, as tens of thousands of people do). His parents bullied him, his friends and mentors bullied him, and the popular press bullied him. The tabloids screamed, 'Don't Dither, Charles!' Even the *Guardian* said that his failure to propose when the press demanded was 'profoundly disappointing for a nation which, beset by economic and political dissent, had briefly believed that the sound of distant tumbrels was to be drowned by the peal of royal wedding bells'. It is revealing that the two previous Princes of Wales were also entirely unable to reconcile their 'duty' to marry with their basic human desire to marry somebody they loved.

Eventually, Charles's father told him to get a move on. Understandably agonised, sensing that Diana might not be right for him, Charles (according to Jonathan Dimbleby) told one of his friends that, 'It is just a matter of taking an unusual plunge into some rather unknown circumstances that inevitably disturbs me, but I expect it will be the right thing in the end.' The night before their wedding, he confessed to Diana that he didn't love her. She said later that as she walked up the aisle watched by a billion people, she was tempted to turn around and run away. Charles himself later admitted that he had wanted to call off the whole thing but was heavily pressured to go through with the wedding. He told Steven Barry how scared he was. Barry explained that, 'It was perfectly clear to me that the Prince's concern was more than a gentleman's collywobbles.'

Charles went to see his mother to express his fears. He told an aide that she showed only stern expectation: 'She wasn't there', he explained. If Charles and Diana had been a normal couple and not part of the monarchy, they could have ended their relationship with comparative ease (if indeed they would ever have got together in the first place). But, as it was, the monarchy forced them onto a path which was to kill one of them and destroy the other.

The tragedy is that it was clear from the very start of Diana's contact with the toxic force of monarchy that it held the potential to destroy her. Her mother, even before the wedding, issued a public statement asking 'whether, in the public execution of their jobs, [journalists] consider it necessary or fair to harass my daughter daily, from dawn until well after dark?' Diana seemed to know before the wedding that she was hurtling towards disaster (although this may have been the wisdom that comes with hindsight). She was told on the eve of the wedding by her Scotland Yard bodyguard, Chief Inspector Paul Officer – a silly name, I know – that, 'This is the last night of freedom in your life, so make the most of it.' She later said that 'those words felt like a sword through my heart'.

Charles's whole life virtually guaranteed that he would never be capable of being a good husband to an averagely needy person, never mind somebody as desperately needy as Diana. One ex-girlfriend of his told the respected Nigel Dempster, 'An awful lot of women who went to bed with him would never have gone to bed with him if he had not been HRH. However badly Sir treats you afterwards – it's a kind of pact: you know that the royal psychology is based on the notion of rule, right? – you only get what you deserve.' How could a man surrounded by very odd women like this – *whose only experience of women is those with this psychology* – be capable of the reciprocity and mutual support essential to a good happy marriage?

Diana's father told her on the eve of her wedding that, 'a prince is condemned to a unique and lifelong loneliness. Don't expect too much in the way of friendship at first.' Diana was expected to behave like a nineteenth-century royal. 'Queen' Victoria's son Bertie married Alexandra, who was expected to simply passively accept the existence of his mistress Alice Keppel (who was Camilla Parker-Bowles' great-grandmother). But Diana was a woman who refused to lie back and think a vibrator was England's future King. (And even Diana, as her butler Paul Burrell informs us, owned such items.) She expected – reasonably enough – to have something approaching a normal marriage; she deserved no less.

It is utterly predictable that the Windsors, obsessed with heredity and birth lines, would try to find an explanation for Diana's 'unruliness' (that is, her disappointment that she could not have a normal marriage) in her family history. John Bowes-Lyon, a relative of the 'Queen

Mother', said before Diana's death that, 'apparently what she suffers from can be hereditary, and there have been other instances in the Fermoy family, so the royal family have been told.' The Queen Mother told Woodrow Wyatt, a leading journalist and friend, that she believed Diana was 'schizophrenic'.

It is true that Diana did begin to show signs of a mental illness of some kind. (Most people do at one point or another.) It would be more surprising if somebody in her position *didn't* show such signs. The kind of attention Diana was subjected to could only serve to warp her totally. Indeed, she became so self-absorbed that she bordered on complete self-obsession. Friends said that she even resented the Falklands War because she felt it was distracting attention from her. But, as her friend Caroline Bartholomew said, 'How could you not be self-obsessed when half the world is watching everything you do?'

We could tie ourselves up for hours in knotty ethical dilemmas about whether the Windsor family, the editors of newspapers or the people who buy newspapers are responsible for these miserable press intrusions. But isn't it better just to cut through these irresolvable rows and simply remove the source of the pictures?

The leaked 'Squidgygate' tapes of Diana speaking to her lover James Gilbey reveal a woman constantly aware of being monitored by the press. 'There aren't that many pictures, are there? There haven't been that many', she says desperately of an outing. Later, she interrupts frantically, 'Did you see the *News of the World*?' She continues, 'I am always smiling, aren't I?' Her perpetual act – what Gilbey describes as being able to 'sense a camera at a thousand yards' – is what made Diana such a successful royal and such a failed human being. The two can only ever go together. Somebody who has adjusted their behaviour to take it for granted that at any moment they might be being spied on is a person who cannot be happy. Yet it is what monarchy requires in the twenty-first century.

The press coverage was so overwhelming that Diana seems to have seriously begun to believe some of the more hyperbolic press claims that she literally had a 'healing touch' bestowed upon her by 'guiding spirits'. All this shows is that normal people thrust into the monarchy become twisted beyond all recognition by the sheer weight and velocity of the institution. When she first entered it, she was comparatively normal. Diana is one of the few Windsors, for example, who had the good sense and egalitarian instincts to find titles and feudal hierarchies silly. She would laugh when people called her 'Ma'am' or 'Your Royal Highness'.

Diana eventually could bear the pressure no more and sued a freelance paparazzo for stalking. She said that, 'he seems to know my every move. I shall suffer undue psychological pressure and become ill.' She was kidding herself, however, that picking off one fish would stave off an ocean of interest in her. There was so much money to be made from selling photos of her that no court order in the world could have prevented paparazzi. Of course, this attention was dangerous (and ultimately lethal). But it was also unstoppable. The always-excellent journalist Matthew Parris was eerily prophetic when, in 1997, he asked if we were 'turning the lives of people like Diana and Charles into what amounts to a snuff soap opera?' Within months, Diana was dead.

Does anybody doubt that Diana Spencer's life would have been immeasurably better if she had never become mixed up with the institution of monarchy?

4

MARGARET

A Character Study of How Monarchy Can Wreck Your Personality

The bizarre, twisted psychology of Margaret Windsor, who sadly died in early 2002, provides us with an important lesson about the monarchy. Her awful life demonstrates the corrosive effects upon the personality of growing up within the royal family.

The world-view Margaret developed was, to put it mildly, a little odd. Examples of her extreme and rancid snobbery are so numerous that this book could consist of nothing but. She insisted that everyone, even her close friends, address her as 'Ma'am', because, she explained, it was 'her due' as royalty. She made her own daughter-in-law curtsy to her every time they met. Margaret refused to say anything to a domestic servant. If she wanted to make a comment about a member of her staff, she would write it down on a silver-edged notepad which she kept near her at all times. She would then pass this to her private secretary who would summon the servant to pass on Margaret's thoughts. One of her friends (it is a miracle she had any) said that, 'she needs to hear the crack of a knee at least three times before breakfast'.

Margaret looked down on everyone who did not have royal status. She insisted that anybody who married into the royal family should 'defer to those born in the purple', and refused to even acknowledge 'Princess' Michael 'of Kent', who merely married into the firm. Margaret said of Peter Townsend's second wife, 'She might be rich, but she's not royal.' She followed proudly in the tradition of Queen Victoria, who participated in a disastrous series of dinners which were intended to introduce her to some of her subjects. In practice, Victoria refused to sit next to anybody who was not royal, and spent almost the entire evening talking only to royalty.

Margaret viewed royalty as genetically superior.

She told her friend Gore Vidal that, 'I detested [my grandmother] Queen Mary. She was rude to all of us except Lillibet, who was going to be Queen. Of course, she [Queen Mary] had an inferiority complex. We were royal, and she was not.' It is not 'Queen' Mary who had the inferiority complex though. Margaret clung obsessively to her royal status, I suspect, because at some level she knew that it was the sole interesting thing about her. Shorn of her title, she would be exposed as nothing but a lazy snob with no recognisable talents or qualities.

Margaret established a series of social protocols surrounding herself which sound like something from a Monty Python sketch. Once she entered a room, nobody was allowed to leave before her – so if she wanted to sit up until four in the morning, everyone else had to wait up too. If any normal person began to experience such ludicrous delusions of grandeur simply because of who her parents were, her friends would soon tell her where to get off, or she would find herself without friends. This is the Darwinian process by which we all learn our social skills. Yet royals – because of the very silly deference which still persists towards them – don't ever go through this learning process. Therefore, they all become quite seriously socially maladjusted.

Monarchy destroyed all of Margaret's personal relationships in an especially cruel way. She was, famously, not allowed to marry the man she loved, Peter Townsend. Just because she fell in love with (whisper it! are you ready to be shocked?) a *divorced* man, the poor woman was subjected to comments like those of Dr Graham Leonard, the Bishop of Truro, who said that, 'Princess Margaret's personal life cannot remain purely a family matter, because what the Monarchy does affects society.' It is these monarchists who were most cruel to Margaret. The MP Willie Hamilton, the best advocate of republicanism in Britain for many decades, merely drew attention to the logic of the monarchists' arguments: he pointed out that as a person paid public money, she was expected to have higher standards. 'That', he explained, 'has always been part of the case of pro-monarchists.' His solution was to set Margaret free to live the decadent life she longed for; the monarchists' solution was to keep her caged. Who was more cruel?

But that's not all. Because of the taboo about a royal divorce, Margaret became trapped for decades in a marriage which sounds eerily similar to Edward Albee's play, *Who's Afraid of Virginia Woolf?* She and her husband Lord Snowdon would write notes to each other with titles like 'Twenty Things I Fucking Hate About You'. One scene, above all, illustrates the mutual torture into which this marriage descended. At a friends' dinner party, Snowdon sat with a paper bag over his head. Nobody said anything for the first course, or the second, until eventually Margaret asked icily why he was wearing it. 'Because I can't stand the fucking sight of you', he replied. If she had not been imprisoned in the institution of monarchy, this torment could have been ended many years before the pair actually did call it a day.

Margaret is a perfect case study of the character-deforming fall-out that results from sitting too close to the radioactive core of the monarchy. The institution is the absolute epicentre of British snobbery. Can we really blame this poor creature, raised as though it was an institution that should be taken seriously, for turning out so abnormal? We have to bear in mind the warped way in which Margaret was raised. As a tiny infant, she had to bid goodnight to her grandfather by curtsying whilst walking backwards while wishing, 'Your Majesty a peaceful night's sleep.' If you raise a child in Chernobyl, do not be surprised if it has birth defects; if you raise a child in the British monarchy, do not be surprised if it grows to think that birth determines worth.

Let's not be too sympathetic to Margaret though. Predictably, her defenders have touted her charity work as evidence of her inherent goodness and the value of monarchy. They have failed to mention, however, the evidence Kitty Kelley uncovered that Margaret often demanded personal appearance fees and first-class accommodation in order to appear at overseas charity events. Her behaviour was so generally obnoxious, in this and in all areas, that even in the much more deferential 1970s, then-MP Denis Canavan said that, 'the Princess is a parasite. She should not get any money at all.' Her greatest achievement in life seems to have been to have successfully got away with doing virtually nothing. In that vein, the ultra-royal maniacs who suggested a public holiday to mark Margaret's funeral were onto something: what better way to mark her life than to give us all a day of paid idleness?

Margaret was a victim of a very English form of abuse. It is monstrously cruel to raise a child to be gawked at throughout their childhood and for all their lives, to deny them the freedom to choose their own partner, their own religion, their own politics ... There is one pathetic (in the true meaning of the word) moment in Woodrow Wyatt's diaries about Margaret. He says that, 'Viscount Linley [her son] said she has always longed to go on a bus. He had promised he would take her one day. She has never been on one. I can see that the security angle could be somewhat difficult.' Can you think of a more pitiful image of how the monarchy divorced

Margaret from reality than a woman in her sixties longing, just once, to be able to travel on a bus? On another occasion, Margaret said it wasn't until she grew up that she realised that everything outside Buckingham Palace didn't smell of fresh paint and new-mown grass.

Her bizarre upbringing is especially sad because, without it, she might well have been a likeable woman. Her desire to live life to the full – especially the admirable stance of taking a twentysomething lover when she was in her forties – is impressive. Almost alone amongst her family, she at least had the nerve to rebel against the stuffiness of some (but far from all) of the social conventions of the 1950s. I wish she could have been rescued from monarchy; but she had a form of Stockholm syndrome, the condition where the victims of kidnapping fall in love with their captors. Margaret became obsessed with monarchy, so much so that she couldn't see that it was destroying her life. Now she's gone, we really ought to be asking whether another generation of kids should be treated the same way.

5

ELIZABETH BOWES-LYON

A Character Study of How Monarchy Can Wreck Your Bank-Balance (And Turn You into a Monster)

I want you to imagine how the *Daily Mail* would describe a purely hypothetical person. This person – let's say she is a woman – is old, very old, and has in the course of her long life racked up far more debt than she could ever dream of repaying (over £3 million), despite the fact that she has never done a day's work. In order to feed her addictions to alcohol and gambling, the old woman not only takes this money from banks knowing she would never repay them, she also scrounges from the British taxpayer week in, week out. The taxpayers' money she greedily races through is many thousands of times greater than the sums paid out to war heroes, who are left to quietly rot in isolation on damp council estates.

Well, you've guessed it: this isn't a fictional character, it's our dear old late Queen Mum. This is a woman whose spending was so decadent that even the ultra-Tory Chancellor Norman Lamont complained that, 'she far exceeds her Civil List and the Treasury gets very het up about it'. She squandered taxpayers' money on indulgences which remain unreported by the Tory press. For example, Woodrow Wyatt, her dear friend, arrived for lunch at her home, Clarence House. He explained that there were 'lashings of servants everywhere, as usual, and standing behind one's chair at luncheon'.

We shouldn't be too harsh on the late Elizabeth Bowes-Lyon though. Her plain character flaws were once again the result of that bizarre institution, the monarchy. Monarchy damaged Elizabeth by giving her a grotesquely warped view of Britain and her own privilege. In Woodrow Wyatt's diaries, for example, she complained to him that it was 'a myth' that the royals were rich or out of touch. She said on one occasion, 'We're not rich at all, not in serious terms.' Another time, she said, 'Look at us, we are just ordinary people – look at us around the table – having an ordinary lunch.' Even Wyatt, whose sycophancy knew no bounds, was forced to note that, 'I don't think ordinary people have a luncheon in a huge London garden with about six liveried footmen wearing medals waiting on them.' Quite.

Her cheerful wasting of our money was breathtaking. For example, in the early 1990s, Michael Peat, a new finance director appointed by the Palace, began to spot crucial areas of wasteful expenditure cropping up all over the place. They could usually be traced back to two offenders: Elizabeth Bowes-Lyon and Charles Windsor. The 'Queen Mother' vehemently resisted any economies. She even insisted that it was a legitimate use of public funds and buildings to maintain the 'Ascot office', whose job is to do nothing but keep a register of members of the Royal Enclosure and send them entry vouchers. (And as it happens, nobody from the Palace will provide figures of how many people work in this office or how much it costs us.) Because of her, our money was until her death still frittered away on this obscene frivolity.

Eighty-three people were employed to look after Elizabeth Bowes-Lyon while she was alive: enough to staff at least two well-equipped high schools educating hundreds of children; enough to staff three accident-and-emergency wards saving thousands upon thousands of people every year. For just one little old lady were provided four footmen, two pages (yes, they really do still have terms like that), three chauffeurs (what did they do, split her into three parts for transportation?), a private secretary, an orderly, a housekeeper and five housemaids. The list goes on and on.

The woman's life was filled with evidence that she relished an entirely unearned deference and an almost comically extreme decadence. She instructed her young daughters to refer to her not as 'Mummy' but as 'the Queen' when others were present. She had her infant children served their nursery food, hilariously, by two scarlet-liveried footmen, and their menu was printed for them in French. The Queen Mother believed that she and her family should have been exempt from paying taxation, as though they lived above British society rather than within it. Robert Fellowes, Elizabeth Windsor's former private secretary, was delegated by Elizabeth to tell her mother of her decision to begin coughing up for the Exchequer. Palace insiders reported that her reaction was incandescent rage. She even opposed the idea of allowing 'commoners' into Buckingham Palace, even if they were allowed to fork out nearly ten pounds and only a few rooms were open for viewing.

Her extraordinary financial wastefulness becomes even more striking when you realise that she was given an awful lot of expensive goods entirely free. She was given all her clothes entirely gratis, for example, and she paid her servants an absolute pittance, cashing in on their 'deference' and the taxpayer-funded 'grace and favour' apartments she could offer.

Ludicrously, the 'Queen Mother' acted as though her money-burning escapades were selfless acts of patriotism. Michael Mann, the former Dean of Windsor who knew her very well, had explained that, 'she has a very high view of the duties of the royal family. She feels that Britain is Great Britain and that, therefore, ours must be no banana court. To lower standards [that is, her spending on champagne, caviar and limousines] is to denigrate the country and, insofar as high standards require big spending, so be it. [Easy to say when it's not your money.] She wants to uphold a great destiny and a great country. If you're going to do that, you have to live in a certain style.'

Elizabeth's conception of the monarchy was, at least, always honestly expressed. She saw it as a big-budget, lavish banquet. She was known to find the smaller-scale monarchies of continental Europe ridiculous, particularly the idea of a 'monarch on a bike'. She never even learned how to ride a bike. She always insisted on a royal limousine to transport her wherever she might need to go.

Perhaps because of this exalted view of monarchy, Elizabeth was determined from a young age to marry into the royal family. She was, to put it kindly, an aggressive social climber.

(French Prime Minister Edouard Daladier met Elizabeth in 1939. He believed her husband was 'a moron' and that Elizabeth was 'an excessively ambitious young woman who would be ready to sacrifice every other country in the world so that she might remain Queen.')

After she tried and failed to court the attractive older brother, she settled for the runt of the litter. This in part explains her wild hatred of her brother-in-law, the Duke of Windsor. As the Duke himself said in an interview, 'To put it politely, she wanted to marry me.'

Her obsession with monarchy clearly derives in part from her belief that heredity entirely determined worth. She always took questions of royal lineage with a seriousness that reveals this twisted world-view. She was much exercised, for example, about the question of whether Philip was 'properly' royal before he married Elizabeth. Some argued that Philip was not a 'proper' royal because his dynasty had fallen from real power. The fact that Elizabeth actually worried about such nonsense reflects badly on her. Her obsession with breeding horses, and her lengthy study of their lineage, is a revealing hobby. Obsessed with heredity as the determinant of value in the royal sphere, this mindset was extended into her recreations too.

We should never forget that she was a woman who was desperate to force herself into a rigid class-based caste system, and she did everything she could once she got there to preserve it in aspic. She told Woodrow Wyatt, 'I hate that classlessness. It is so unreal.' And in her world of butlers, courtiers and bowing and scraping, it must have seemed that classlessness really was depressingly unreal. Wyatt also provides us with a revealing anecdote of Elizabeth's vile snobbery. An old friend who hadn't seen her in ages rushed up to her to embrace her, and she said, 'Harry, remember who I am and who you are.'

All of the language surrounding Elizabeth Bowes-Lyon is saturated with class prejudice. She found it hard to understand why Diana Spencer went off the rails when she was 'from a good family', meaning an aristocratic family. The implication is that non-aristocratic families are somehow 'bad'.

This is just one of many deeply unpleasant aspects to this bitter old woman. Her politics can only be described as far right. She was, for example, an avid supporter of white minority rule in Rhodesia. Paul Callan of the *International Express* says, 'She is not fond of black folk.' She revealed to Wyatt that she had 'some reservations about Jews'. She made it publicly known, when she was Queen, that she regretted the end of Britain's colonial occupation of India. One of her ladies-in-waiting has explained that her attitude to Africa was, 'Poor darlings. The Africans just don't know how to govern themselves – it's just not their form. What a pity we're not still looking after them.' She has rather accurately been described by a former courtier as 'an up-market Alf Garnett'.

This is not simply unpleasant. It has had massive repercussions on the history of Britain. It is easily forgotten now, but Elizabeth was one of the staunchest supporters of appeasing Adolf Hitler. She bent over backwards to use her influence to stop Britain going to war against the Nazis, and she saw Churchill as a dangerous ally of her brother-in-law Edward. When Chamberlain returned, famously, with Hitler's meaningless promise that he would not provoke a war, Elizabeth made the constitutionally unprecedented decision to appear alongside Chamberlain on the Buckingham Palace balcony, thus putting her personal stamp of approval on the obscene policy of appeasing fascism.

But her unsavoury characteristics didn't even end there. One of the facets of Elizabeth's character which comes through again and again in honest accounts of her is her hatred of the weak. Her sick cousins were packed off to asylums and never spoken of again. She even lied in her *Who's Who* entry, simply pretending that they didn't exist. Whenever her daughters were ill, she didn't want to know. She despised Diana's work with AIDS victims and lepers, because she found the sight of a Princess mixing with the palpably inferior embarrassing.

She came to despise her own weaknesses too. She hated it when people asked how she was, and her staff had been known to warn people not to refer to her recent ailments. She would not wear glasses, despite the fact that because of this she could by the time of her death barely read or write. The 'Queen Mother' had even been known to ignore a fever of 103 degrees so that she could keep an appointment at Cheltenham. To admit to her temperature would have been to concede that she was somehow inferior. The Nietzschean streak to her character is obvious. Elizabeth cared only for the strong, the rich and the powerful. Anybody else had to fall to the wayside and quietly rot out of her line of vision.

Yet, with an acquiescent press, Elizabeth – remarkably – managed to present herself as somebody with 'the common touch'. This derives primarily from the one achievement of her entire life – her decision to remain in London during the Blitz, and not flee to the safety of Canada. It is true that this was an admirable choice, but it is often described in disingenuous terms. She claimed that, once Buckingham Palace was bombed, she could 'look the East End in the face'. But as Ben Pimlott explains, 'the East End was not able to retreat to Windsor to catch up on sleep, or to spend recuperative holidays in Norfolk and Scotland. Nor was the East End able to supplement its diet with pheasants and venison shot on the royal estates.'

Elizabeth was so far from being 'one of us' that it is hard to put the economic and social gap into words. Suffice it to say that she had always been surrounded by servants; her parents were 'Lord' and 'Lady' Strathmore, and from birth she was waited on by a gaggle of servants including a butler, two footmen, five housemaids, a cook and numerous room maids. She grew up with four palaces at her disposal.

So, yes, she went from being a 'commoner' to a 'royal' – but she wasn't exactly a terribly common commoner. In fact, what is most striking when you read biographies of the Queen Mother is just how little she ever did. Apart from staying in London during (most of) the Blitz, it's extraordinary to find that in fact, decade after decade, she did literally nothing of note at all. In most ordinary lives, there are heroic acts (not least raising children, something the Queen Mother delegated away), funny lines, amusing tales. From Elizabeth Bowes-Lyon, despite her exalted social position, there was an embarrassing silence.

Indeed this is so pointed that pro-monarchists have been forced to turn this limpid lack of achievement into a fortune. W.F. Deedes, the legendary *Telegraph* columnist who has also impressed everyone with his sheer longevity, claimed that, 'In an increasingly earnest world, she teaches us all how to have fun, that life should not be all about learning, earning and resting. In a world where we have all become workaholics, there she is grinning at racehorses. She reminds us that there is life beyond sex, shopping and soccer. [What – horses?] Bless her heart.' He is not as generous when he describes dole claimants who have chosen not to work. They are evil 'scroungers'; they aren't just reminding us of the value of non-work activities. This is despite the fact that they take only a tiny, tiny fraction of the 'Queen Mother's' claims from the public purse.

Many people admired the fact that she

survived so long. It's true that an elderly lady who still lives life to the full is worthy of admiration. I have no doubt that the vast majority of old ladies would also love to be kept constantly stimulated by a small army whose job is solely to entertain them. I have no doubt that virtually every pensioner could live to be a centenarian if they had never eaten anything but the best food, been cared for by the best doctors, and lived in the most lavish Palaces. So don't give Elizabeth kudos just for surviving in an environment which could bring virtually any person hobbling through into a fresh millennium.

Some people admired the fact that Elizabeth, as they put it, 'likes a drink'. Well, yes, she was clearly an alcoholic. Graham Turner's authoritative profile describes her as drinking gin before meals and champagne during them. All of them. An old friend of hers explained, 'I knew she likes a big gin and Dubonnet, so I gave her a whopper, which I suppose amounted to a triple, and then went round to the other people. When I came back to her, four or five minutes later, her glass was already empty. "So delicious," she said, "perhaps just a little more." She has three of those triples before lunch and her fair share of wine during it. Yet, afterwards, she walked briskly for several hundred yards in a straight line.'

There is nothing necessarily wrong with being an alcoholic. I have known a number of highly functional alcoholics who are aware that they are destroying their livers but are doing no harm to anybody else, and are perfectly capable of holding down part-time jobs. So I do not condemn the Queen Mother's alcoholism. I must admit, however, that I find it slightly worrying (and indicative of our extremely juvenile attitude towards alcohol in this country) that we seem to actually see her alcoholism as something to admire. It isn't. It's a sad reality, nothing more. Yet in the absence of any other recognisable qualities, the defenders of monarchy have had to pull the rather desperate stunt of praising the 'Queen Mother' on the grounds that she was an alcoholic.

Perhaps Elizabeth does have one towering achievement though: conning us into the belief that she was a nice old dame. In fact, the 'Queen

Mother', far from being the simple 'wifie' of popular myth, was a cunning Machiavellian manipulator. One aristocratic friend of Elizabeth, Philippa de Pass, says that, 'She could give a few lessons in statecraft to Machiavelli. People think she is simply a charming and adorable old lady, but she's a tiger.' At the height of the abdication crisis, she developed a highly convenient 'flu' which confined her to her bed and kept her out of the public eye so she could seem to return, triumphant and unsullied, when it was all over and she and her husband were needed. Many of her friends openly praise her for her plotting at this time. Patricia Mountbatten correctly describes her as 'the iron fist in the velvet glove'.

Marian Crawford quotes Elizabeth as saying, 'We are not supposed to be human.' She without doubt accordingly cultivated a cruel inhumanity towards her relatives. She despised her sister-in-law, Wallis Simpson, and many believe that she 'helped put the bullets in the gun' when Edward and Wallis were destroyed. When the Duke of Windsor died, Elizabeth did not allow her vendetta against Wallis Simpson, his partner, abate. The American (whose greatest crime, we should remember, was to get divorced and fall in love again) was invited to stay at Buckingham Palace only for the duration of the funeral. As soon as the ceremony was over, Elizabeth ordered her family to head off to Windsor and thus leave Simpson alone at the Palace. This casual vindictiveness to a grieving woman is not reported by the pro-monarchy press, because they know that it would shatter their deceitful projection of a kindly old lady.

But her cruelty is not only directed towards the mourning. Elizabeth ordered the Palace switchboard to turn away any calls from Edward. Apart from a very brief return to Britain for his mother's funeral in 1953, Edward was permanently exiled from his own country by Elizabeth. She had a similarly callous reaction to the death of Diana Spencer (the mother of her great-grandchildren). Graham Turner, a very sympathetic *Telegraph* journalist who greatly admires the woman, nonetheless revealed that, a few days after Diana's awful death in Paris, the

Queen Mother told a guard that he was 'very wise' for saying that there was 'some good' in this situation: William and Harry would no longer be pulled in two directions at once.

The monarchy made her so filled with admiration for the institution that she began to heartlessly abuse the individuals at its core. Her first thought when Diana died was not for the feelings of her grandchildren but for an abstract constitutional form. What sort of monster did monarchy turn Elizabeth Bowes-Lyon into?

6

PHILIP MOUNTBATTEN

The Provider of Semen

Philip Mountbatten is of a generation in which men expected to be Men. So he has found the life of courtier to a monarch humiliating, degrading and miserable. A courtier very close to the couple said to royal journalist Nigel Dempster, 'One must recognise the sheer unreasonableness of having a wife in such an overwhelmingly superior position to her husband as the Queen is to Philip. What other man in the world must swear to be his wife's liegeman [oh, the humiliation!], and walk two paces behind her? Ostensibly, he's the head of the family, but when the chips are down, his wife is always the Queen.'

We might balk at the palpable sexism (and

perhaps even misogyny) evident here – after all, this courtier would, I suspect, be little worried about the superiority of a King to his wife. But this is the sexist world which Philip has always inhabited, and it is these values that he shares. He feels the shame keenly. For him, it was particularly degrading that his children took his wife's surname and not his own. He said that, 'I am the only man in the country who isn't allowed to give his name to his children.'

He has also found it deeply depressing that the monarchy forced him to give up his job. Again, that generation of men defined themselves entirely by their work. But Philip was allowed to have no meaningful work at all. When he spoke in 1993 to a journalist from the *Independent on Sunday*, he said, 'It wasn't my ambition to be President of the Mint Advisory Committee. I didn't want to be President of the World Wildlife Fund. I was asked to do it. I'd much rather have stayed in the Navy, frankly.' All of Philip's friends confirm the extent to which this cruel blow really damaged his life. Lady Kennard, a close friend of Philip (and, for once, that isn't a euphemism for mistress), explains that, 'In the beginning [of Elizabeth's reign] he had a very hard time ... He had been through a war and he wanted nothing more than to remain in the Navy. It wasn't to be, of course.'

One person who was present when Philip found out that Elizabeth had just become Queen said, 'I'll never forget it. He looked as if half the world had just fallen in on him.' Another said, 'He sat slumped behind a copy of *The Times*. He didn't want it at all. It was going to change his whole life: take away the emotional stability he'd just found.' Philip had always wanted to be an admiral, but realised then that this dream had to die. He became deeply depressed and would spend many hours locked away, alone, brooding.

When Philip first married into the royal family, he was a dynamic, thrusting reformer. He was impatient with the stuffy, courtier-led ways of the Palace. But eventually this spirit was eroded away, and his energy simply curdled into a rancid bitterness. He is now considered to be one of the most conservative members of the family, and the least willing to change the institutions.

That bitterness might well be the source of his endless embarrassing insults to people of seemingly every nationality. Philip's charming comments have included telling the Egyptians that they 'breed too much', telling a British tourist in Budapest that, 'You can't have been here too long; you aren't pot-bellied' and telling British students in China that, 'If you stay here much longer, you'll get slitty eyes.' He even said to a woman in Kenya who handed him a gift, 'You are a woman, aren't you?' There seems to be more than a hint of anger in these comments. Philip said in 1967, 'I'm sick of making excuses for this country.' We might well say the same to you, Philip.

Some argue that these comments, as well as being simply offensive, also reveal an unpleasantly hard-right political bias. Prince Philip's brother-in-law was an SS colonel who worked closely with the arch-racist and genocidal maniac Heinrich Himmler. His other three sisters all married pro-Nazi Princes. Philip himself, of course, fought bravely in a war against fascism – but nonetheless, his sisters' choices indicate at least that Philip grew up in a family that was comfortable with the most extreme and poisonous kinds of racism. One MP, William Gallagher, said at the time of Philip's wedding that he was 'sure he has not forsaken the family politics'. This view is lent credence by the fact that Philip once told the Paraguayan dictator General Stroessner that, 'It's a pleasant change to be in a country that isn't ruled by its people.'

If Philip kept his political views to himself, they would be distasteful but irrelevant. As it is, he is married to a person who takes key decisions about the government of Britain. It is worrying, then, that he has often intruded into politics in unpleasant ways. Even the ultra-right-wing MP Enoch Powell was once prompted to complain about Philip when the Duke sat in the House of Commons gallery and loudly commented on the MPs' speeches. After the horrific Dunblane massacre, Philip publicly opposed government policy to reduce massively the number of guns in private hands, saying, 'If a cricketer, for instance, suddenly decided to go into a school and batter a lot of people to death with a cricket bat, which he could do very easily, I mean, are you going to ban cricket bats?' Several parents of the children murdered said they found his comments deeply upsetting.

This combines with Philip's warped view of his own privilege to give an unfavourable impression of the man. He said in 1981, at the height of a recession which led to millions of people becoming unemployed, 'Everyone was saying we must have more leisure. Now they are complaining they are unemployed.' He has also denied that there is any poverty in Britain.

Yet he believes, seriously, that the royal family are financially deprived. In an interview in 1970 with the American TV show 'Meet the Press', he lamented – clearly expecting sympathy – that the royal family's finances were in trouble, and said self-pityingly, 'We may need to move into smaller premises, who knows?' (He did not say which of the four massive palaces he occupies might have to be replaced with 'smaller premises'.) He also said that – get your tissues ready here – he had already had to sell a small yacht (can you imagine the agony?) and might even *have to give up polo.* This was from a man so bitingly poor that he owns a fully-equipped barbershop retained for his exclusive use.

Philip plainly, therefore, has a rather odd view of British society. His decisions about schooling his children (and they were exclusively *his* decisions, with little input from his wife) reveal even more about how he views us common folk. He felt that a normal state school would be far beneath his child. Indeed, his Palace advisors said that the teachers working in these slums would 'be more likely to be overawed by their responsibility' than those with experience of the aristocracy, and that fellow pupils 'drawn from the humbler strata of society' would be quite unable to cope with this 'fabulous animal' in their midst.

This shows that Philip and his courtiers saw Britain as a class pyramid with the royals at its top and several layers of aristocrats and upper-middle-class types insulating them from the barbarians at its base. They still see Britain this way. We know this because virtually all the royal private secretaries are from Eton, and those few who aren't are still reliable members of the 'old boy's network'. (Of course, none of them are black or Asian. That would be simply *too* vulgar.)

Indeed, the entire Windsor family move only within a tiny aristocratic élite which they see as a 'buffer' between themselves and the common hoard of unwashed peasants. Diana, for example, met Charles because her elder sister had had an affair with him, her other sister is married to the Queen's Private Secretary, her father was an Equerry to the Queen and her father, her grandmother was a Woman of the Bedchamber (yes, that's a real job) to the Queen Mother, and so on. There are countless other examples – Princess Anne romanced Andrew Parker-Bowles, who married Camilla, who was sleeping with Charles ... The smallness of the aristocratic club surrounding the royals is plain.

Philip's eventual choice of school for his eldest son is also fascinating. The journalist Peregrine Worsthorne described Gordonstoun as 'an institution which is fully classless', a view similar to his friend Philip's. It is a telling detail that Philip thought a school which cost *more* than Eton, and which schooled almost exclusively the children of millionaires, to be classless.

Philip's unpleasant characteristics don't end there. He has also shown a worrying love of slaughtering endangered species. On one shooting trip in the 1960s, for example, he shot a tiger, a crocodile and a rhinoceros. Before anybody writes to me to say that standards were different then, I should point out that in fact there was a widespread public uproar *at the time*. It seems rather odd that he considers this behaviour consistent with being President of the World Wildlife Fund.

Even Philip's more likeable activities can serve only to expose the awfulness of monarchy as an institution. For example, Philip in the 1950s raided the 'treasure house' of art works which belong to the nation but which were kept hoarded away unseen in Palace cellars. He allowed some of the 'lesser pieces' to be used in the rooms of the domestic staff. In some ways, this is an act of kindness, and Philip should be praised. Yet it can only stir the anger of anyone who opposes hereditary privilege: what right have Philip Mountbatten and the Windsor family to the better pieces simply because of birth, whilst the 'lesser' items are palmed off on people just as good (if not better) than them, who just happen to have been born 'below stairs'?

Few people deny that monarchy has made Philip miserable. Unable to have a satisfying job, subjugated to (shock! horror!) a woman, he has found it difficult to cope, taking comfort in many close female friends. He has had an empty life. It might seem rude to point this out – but you know that if it were the other way round, he'd say far worse about you.

7

CHARLES

A Character Study of How Monarchy Can Wreck Almost Everything About You

Charles, more than any other royal except perhaps Margaret, has had his life ruined by the monarchy. The monarchy has put Charles in a uniquely savage position. He can only prepare for one job, but he can't do that job until he is an old man. Indeed, it must have crossed his mind that he might *never* get to be monarch at all. His grandmother outlived one of her children; his mother, who seems likely to repeat that longevity, may well outlive him. Charles has always been acutely aware of the trap he's in. As he told an audience at Cambridge University when he was in his twenties, 'My great problem in life is that I do not really know what my role in life is. At the moment I do not have one. But somehow I must find one.'

Charles's frustration at not having a job is so intense that he has on occasion wished his own mother dead. He approached his then brother-in-law, Charles Spencer, at the funeral of Diana's father, and repeatedly told him how lucky he was to have inherited so young. He then added, 'I wish I had inherited young.'

From birth, Charles has never been treated like a normal child. Lord Mountbatten said that, 'Loneliness is something that royal children have always suffered and always will. Not much you can do about it really.' This was callous but true. Charles found it hard to make friends. He was taken to primary school every day in a royal limousine, greeted at the gate by a bowing headmaster, and seen off by him at the end of the day too. His childhood was filled with bizarre special treatment. For example, it was judged that it would be terribly vulgar for a Prince to use a normal, common persons' swimming pool, so for his school swimming lessons, his whole class was taxied to Buckingham Palace. When he started secondary school, the treatment was even worse: on his first day, he was greeted by a crowd of members of the public gawking at him.

At every traumatic moment in Charles's life, the ceaseless glare of the media has made the experience even worse. Every child finds their first day at school unsettling – how much more so must it have been, given that he was also accompanied by yelling hoards of photographers screaming his name all the way to the entrance? All of Charles's rites of passage were splashed across the front pages. When he ordered a cherry brandy in a pub (moderate behaviour indeed for a fifteen-year-old), it caused a press furore that lasted weeks. When he was sixteen, a book of his essays was stolen and published in the German press. The pressure on Charles even at primary school was so intense that by the end of his first term, his headmaster complained that press intrusion was seriously impairing the functioning of his whole school.

In the biographies of all royals, there is a moment when the awfulness of their fate becomes apparent to them. For Charles, it occurred when he was nine years old and he was summoned to his headmaster's study. He was told to watch the television. His mother announced before a baying crowd that she was making her son into the Prince of Wales 'today'. As Jonathan Dimbleby, who is a close friend of the Prince, explains, there was a 'look of acute embarrassment which flashed across the face of the Prince. For him, it was not a moment to rejoice but the sealing of the inevitable, that "awful truth" from which there was no escape.' What parent would put their nine-year-old child through this anguish? And what parent would do it without even warning him in advance, or calling him to offer comfort?

But then, we should bear in mind that Charles was a victim of shocking abuse as a child, which makes even this casual neglect seem slight. His parents, we must never forget, abandoned him for six months when he was only five years old. They often didn't bother to see him on his birthdays even when he was very little. When he was in their company, the Prince was – according to interviews which he himself has given – treated with appalling cruelty by his father, who, according to his biographer Jonathan Dimbleby, would 'seem intent not merely on correcting the Prince but mocking him as well, so that he seemed to be foolish and tongue-tied in front of friends as well as family. To their distress and embarrassment, the small boy was frequently brought to tears [by his father].'

But even this cruelty was not due only to the twisted personality of Philip Mountbatten but also to the institution of monarchy. One friend of Philip explains that, 'Philip hectored his son because it was the only means he knew to achieve his supreme objective – to mould a Prince for kingship.' Another says that, 'Philip put his loyalty to the Crown above and beyond his responsibilities as a father.' So this is yet another significant way in which monarchy has broken Charles Windsor's self-esteem and purpose in life.

Charles has been used since childhood as a PR puppet for the monarchy, a process his parents only encouraged. As the *Daily Mirror* columnist Cassandra wrote when, barely out of his teens, the Prince was subject to a preposterous 'investiture' ceremony: 'He is to be turned into a puppet, publicly in front of all our eyes and ears ... I find myself extremely sorry for Charles, principal boy in the pantomime at Carnarvon next July that should never have been ballyhooed at all: a young man who is already the plaything of outmoded politicians.' But this cruelty stretched right back to his childhood, when he was paraded by his parents before cameramen.

Treated brutally at home, he was sent to a school which can only be described without hyperbole as a centre of sadism. At Gordonstoun, the journalist Ross Benson recalls, the windows would be kept open all night, so that pupils who were forced to sleep next to them 'were likely to wake up with blankets rain-soaked or, in winter, covered with a light sprinkling of snow'. But this was the least of the problems pupils faced. Once lights were out, gangs of thugs would 'roam the house beating up smaller boys, extorting food and money ... and creating an atmosphere of "genuine terror".' New boys would be greeted 'by taking a pair of pliers to their arms and twisting until the flesh tore open'.

Charles was singled out for especially vicious treatment. Lads would deliberately attack him and then brag, 'We did him over. We just punched the future King of England.' Nobody would befriend him for fear of being accused of sucking up. When Charles told the headmaster that he had had his head forced into a toilet pan, he was told to stop being such a sissy.

Parents who failed to notice that their child was being abused in this way would be culpably negligent; Elizabeth and Philip were not. They were worse: they knew everything that was going on, and they did nothing. He wrote to them constantly, explaining that it was 'absolute hell' and that, to give but one example, 'I don't get any sleep practically at all nowadays ... [The people in my dorm] throw slippers all night long or hit me with pillows or rush across the room and hit me as hard as they can ... Last night was hell, literal hell.' But parents who had abandoned him as a child were happy to abandon him again now.

One of Charles's few precious moments of freedom from misery and control was when he was seventeen. Following his trip to a remote community in Australia, a nun wrote that, 'It was grand to see him walking around Dogura – walking alone with no gaping crowds waiting for him ... I do not suppose there are many opportunities for such times in his life.' She said that he had 'come amongst them as if in a cage', which, of course, he was. And even during those years, he was stricken with the knowledge that his parents still didn't care. They didn't even bother to meet the family he was travelling out to Australia with and going to live with for six months.

When he returned from Australia, the cage door snapped shut. He was given almost no freedom to chart the next decade of his own life. In 1965, a committee was set up to decide the Prince's future. The Prime Minister and the Archbishop of Canterbury were on the committee, but Charles himself was not. They decided that he 'would have to enter one of the armed services', but that he should go to university first. Charles was eventually informed about their decisions. He was given no input at all.

Predictably, the decisions they made were grossly inappropriate for the 'Prince'. He was far too unintelligent to go to Cambridge University, and he was almost comically incompetent in the Navy. He couldn't for the life of him master navigation (a pretty fundamental skill when you're at sea), but they couldn't punish his failures in the way they would with anybody else. As the Naval Secretary to the Ministry of Defence wrote, 'the thought of Court Martialling the heir to the throne for a navigational error is good nightmare material'. In the end, he had to be given intensive course after intensive course until eventually he was receiving one-to-one tuition.

It was cruel to put an unintelligent man in positions like this, where he was bound to fail. Yet this points to perhaps the greatest cruelty of all. Charles has been surrounded by sycophants all his life. They have indulged his every whim, including the strange delusion that he is an intelligent man. This has gone on for so long that Charles Windsor now seems seriously to believe that he is an important thinker. A friend of his told Nigel Dempster, the journalist, that, 'he lives in an isolation ward of flattery. He goes to Hollywood and is told he's handsome. He swaps jokes with a comic genius like Peter Sellers and the other Goons, and they fall down laughing. He boffs a woman once, and she tells him he's the greatest lover she's ever had ... The best education in the world can't defend you against sycophancy on that scale.' This process has warped Charles in innumerable ways; the saddest is that it has led him to believe he is intelligent and well-informed.

Yet in truth, Charles has always been of highly questionable intelligence. Even Dimbleby admits that 'he was by no means an apt pupil' at school. Despite some of the most expensive education money can buy, he sat only two A-levels, and in those he achieved the mediocre grades of a B in history and a C in French. He then attended Cambridge University, despite the fact that his grades were nowhere near good enough to merit admission. Predictably, his degree was a disaster, and he came out the other end with a polite 2.2, a qualification which one Cambridge don recently described as being given only to ‘the terminally lazy or the very stupid indeed’.

Even Charles’s closest aides admit that all too often he simply spouts whatever the last person to whisper in his ear has said. Dimbleby admits that, ‘they were uncomfortable with his tendency to reach instant conclusions on the basis of insufficient thought’. Edward Adeane, Charles’s private secretary for many years, was deeply disturbed by the fact that Charles ‘was extraordinarily easy to lead by the nose’. These are understatements.

Charles is as profoundly unintelligent as his mother and grandfather. The difference is that they at least seemed to know that they were hardly Stephen Hawking and acted accordingly. His wife Diana cheerfully admitted that she was ‘thick as two short planks’, but she had other qualities that counted. Charles, in sharp contrast, has (to use A.N. Wilson’s useful term) no intellectual humility at all. Can you imagine him ever being as self-aware about his intelligence as Diana, who, after she bumped into a wall beam and he told her to mind her head, asked, ‘Why? There’s nothing in it!’

His stupidity can be illustrated in countless ways, but let's start with his dire judgement in selecting mentors. Look, for example, at the exceptionally odd 'Lord Mountbatten', from whom Charles constantly sought guidance. Elizabeth Windsor described him as 'a medieval matchmaker', and he certainly seems to have been obsessed to an unhealthy extent with attaching himself to the royal family. He would constantly boast about his (unreal) closeness to Elizabeth. He became obsessed with genealogy (the only integer of merit, according to the Windsors), and his biographer Philip Ziegler explains that he only ever picked up a book if it was about this topic. We can only speculate now about the deep character flaws which led to this desperation. What we can say firmly is that it reveals a lot about Charles that he was drawn to such an unsavoury figure.

Exhibit B in the case of the *People vs. Charles* choice of mentors can be summarised in four words: Laurens van der Post. Charles revered Van der Post as a guru and epitome of all he admired. He took his books away with him on honeymoon, to Diana's dismay. (She took only

Danielle Steel, to Charles's anger – but her novels probably have more basis in fact than Van der Post's purported non-fiction.) Charles wined and dined him, and made great efforts to boost Van der Post's public standing. He even became William's godfather. As Van der Post's distinguished official biographer J.D.F. Jones puts it, 'for twenty years, they shared the most intimate conversations and correspondence. Charles even told him about his dreams.'

Yet Van der Post was, as Jones says, 'a compulsive fantasist'. Amongst his many, many lies were his claims to have an aristocratic lineage, a glittering war career, remarkable political achievements (he claimed, entirely falsely, that he was the author of the 1980 Rhodesia settlement) ... the list goes on.

For those who had any intelligence, the evidence was there. Van der Post admitted, for god's sake, in one of his books that, 'This is one of the problems for me: stories are more completely real to me than life in the here and now. A really true story has transcendent reality for me which is greater than the reality of life.'

Translation: I am a compulsive liar with no regard for the truth.

Yet still his portrait hangs in Charles's study. Under the influence of this charismatic but manifestly dishonest man, Charles allowed himself to be persuaded that Nelson Mandela was not the right man to be elected President of South Africa! Van der Post intoxicated Charles in particular with his tales of the 'noble savages' who lived in the Kalahari. These condescending myths had long since been discredited by anthropologists (something Charles really ought to have known since he studied the subject at university). Yet Van der Post claimed that the African peoples 'participated so deeply' in the life of 'animals, stones and rocks' that 'the experience could almost be called mystical'. Charles lapped up this gibberish.

It is hardly surprising, I suppose, that Charles, with such an underdeveloped intellect, was attracted to Van der Post's rhetoric, which stated that intellectual approaches to life were flawed and missed some unseeable, mystical 'truth' which we can only sense through the trees. Van der Post said that, 'We behave as if there were some magic in mere thought, and we use thinking for purposes for which it was never designed'. Charles kneeled in obeisance before this cascade of tripe. Indeed, Charles tried, rather dismally, to develop this line of thought himself. He told an audience of bemused Harvard graduates that, 'we have concentrated on the development of the intellect to the detriment of the development of the spirit'. This facile dichotomy, between the recognisable intellect and the vacuous spirit, must have been a great temptation for Charles. After all, people could point out that his intellect was painfully deficient, but who could say that his 'spirit' (whatever that might mean) was below par?

Van der Post went even further with this quackery and convinced Charles that the Old Man of Lochnagar, a fictional character that Charles had created when he was twenty in a story for his little brothers, was Charles's 'guru' inherited through the ages and embedded in Charles's 'collective unconscious'. How that old charlatan Van der Post must have chuckled at the extraordinary gullibility of the man.

But then Charles has always been wide open to cranks. In the 1970s, a young Indian woman persistently called Buckingham Palace begging to be put through to Charles. Eventually, she spoke to him and explained that she had a mission as a Buddhist to convert him to understanding the role of the Past Masters. Rather than shrug her off as a madwoman, he invited her into the Palace and formed a friendship with her. She even converted him to vegetarianism.

But there is a common thread running through the lunatics and charlatans that Charles is attracted to. They all articulate some kind of ultra-reactionary hatred of modern life, and the desire to retract to a pre-modern, pre-industrial world. Van der Post, for example, was part of a wider movement which sought to oppose urban life and its cosmopolitan values, and replace it with a vision of a pure, 'natural' life in the jungles, deserts and forests. Van der Post dishonestly claimed that, 'By merely taking the most sophisticated people into the bush and wilds of Africa, we have produced the most startling re-educative and therapeutic effects upon their divided personalities.'

From thinkers like this – and Charles's own endless speeches – we can start to piece together a vision of Charles's political philosophy. Of course, describing Charles's thought is difficult because it is so shallow, facile and at times incoherent: we aren't talking Bertrand Russell here. Nonetheless, there are recurring themes and leitmotifs. Charles is essentially a feudal thinker. Feudalism was the prevailing social structure before capitalism, and it is based on a mystical notion that everybody knows their place within nature. Feudal thinkers believe that we are each born within a particular part of the social hierarchy where we 'belong' and are destined to remain. Monarchy is the archetypal feudal institution. It is central to the thought of the 'old right' which has been so entirely eclipsed during the twentieth century by the new right and the left.

It shouldn't surprise us that a man raised to believe that the feudal institution of monarchy is all-important has turned out to be attracted to long-dead feudal political ideas too. Charles not only aspires to head a feudal institution, he also lives like a feudal lord. Dimbleby says of him that as a landowner, 'he knew all the tenants, the farm workers and their families, their names, their histories and their lives'. Just like the old Lords of the Manor were expected to before those new-fangled ideas like capitalism and equality of opportunity came along …

To find a Western feudal political thinker who is taken seriously, we have to go back to the first Prime Minister of the twentieth century, Lord Salisbury. Andrew Roberts' definitive biography shows that, like Charles, Salisbury was sceptical of industrialisation and idealised the countryside and aristocratic pursuits as somehow more in tune with nature than the vulgar, egalitarian world of the city. The public voice in Britain closest to Charles is the hard-right quarterly, the *Salisbury Review*. Like him, they often fulminate about the lack of Shakespeare in our schools, the arcane question of which should be the authorised prayer book, the state of the countryside, and various other reactionary obsessions. Charles even used his privileged position to lobby the Prime Minister with the odd idea that all teenagers should be sentenced to community service.

Charles and the *Review*, in keeping with their feudalism, venerate Nature (it is always capitalised) as the ultimate good. Often, this simply takes the form of quasi-mystical verbiage dressed up as though it were an intelligent comment. For example, he has uttered the following amusing sentence: 'It is high time we once again respected flights of the spirit; high time we concentrated our collective efforts on unleashing the vast transforming and regenerative potential which lies within the individual as a member of the community.' What can he possibly mean? Does he even know?

This anti-modern instinct can be positively pernicious when it comes to an analysis of developing countries. He said of the economic development of Africa, 'Is all this development really progress?' What? Things like clean water and sewers and all that? Well, yes, actually, you fool. Charles spoke dismissively of the 'squalid little houses' of African towns, from the comfort of his five palaces.

His ascription of special, nostalgic powers to non-European peoples is always offensive, but at times hilarious too. At a Commonwealth dinner in the 1980s, Charles made the following entry in his diary: 'I saw [all the Western delegates making awkward small-talk] while the others [from non-Western countries] merely sat and contemplated the infinite by looking straight through the person sitting opposite them .... I sometimes wonder whether the people who sit throughout ... three hours of dinner without uttering scarcely a word [*sic*] are in fact picking up some kind of thought transference from their neighbours by remaining silent? Slowly but surely I am beginning to indulge in little periods of silence.' Could this entry be parodied?

Further evidence of Charles's exaltation of that nebulous concept, 'nature', and those who he judges to be 'close' to it, can be found in a speech he delivered in 1982 in which he said that doctors 'should be intimate with Nature'. It has also led to an obsession with unproven 'alternative medicine' techniques. Michael Baum, the Professor of Surgery at King's College Hospital

School of Medicine, pointed out that the treatments Charles cited approvingly had nothing but 'anecdotal case-reports' to back them up. Baum warned of 'the tragic consequences of adopting therapeutic revolutions on the basis of a plausible scientific hypothesis in advance of its scientific testing'. Normally a mild man, Baum was provoked to say that Charles was 'guilty of the most extreme intellectual arrogance, or more charitably, of confusing fiction with fact'. John Diamond, the journalist who was dying of cancer, took particular offence at Charles's false claim that there were effective 'alternative' therapies for cancer, and took care in his final months to demolish Charles's offensive lies.

Charles had dabbled in mysticism and non-scientific 'spiritualist' thought before. He had been drawn to parapsychology as a student. He saw it as an occultist school of thought which believes in a 'super-natural' magic that can stretch as far as summoning angels. Nor did he keep these odd beliefs private: he even wrote to a university vice-chancellor urging him to establish a Chair of Parapsychology, describing it as 'of immense significance in terms of the "invisible" aspects of our existence in this universe'. Again, he never questioned whether it was inappropriate for him to use a hereditary, non-merit-based position to seek to influence public affairs in this way.

Following the death of his close confidante Lord Mountbatten, Charles became deeply attracted to the Buddhist actress Zoe Sallis. She gave him the book *The Path of the Masters* and became determined to make him believe in reincarnation. He began to speculate about how Mountbatten might be reincarnated. (The Prince's private secretary, Edward Adeane, intervened and told the Prince that he simply was not free to believe what he chose: he was destined to be head of the Church of England – another cruelty monarchy has inflicted upon him.) He tried to link all these beliefs in with his feudal politics, in what can only be described as an intellectual mishmash which resembled a traffic pile-up. But to him, it all looked perfectly consistent.

There has, however, been one clear thread

running through all his arguments: his clear desire to disparage and insult atheists at every opportunity. He told an audience at the Salvation Army centennial that, 'what we should be worried about is whether people are going to become atheists, whether they are going to be given an idea of what is right or wrong [he implies, extremely insultingly, that the two are linked and that therefore atheists don't know right from wrong] ... These are the things that matter.'

Charles's intellectual arrogance (an odd quality for a man with no intellect) also emerged in his contribution to the 'debate' about the English language. He said that he and others 'wonder what it is about our country and our society that our language has become so sloppy and so limited that we have arrived at wastelands of banality, cliché and casual obscenity'. He added that 'all the people in my office, they can't speak English properly, they can't write English properly. All the letters sent from my office I have to correct myself.'

In no other speech has the corrupting

influence of monarchy on Charles Windsor been more clear. He does not have a good or even adequate grasp of English himself. His own writing is, to use his own phrase, filled with banality and cliché, and his speech is itself filled with casual obscenity (fancy being a Tampax, anyone?). I strongly suspect that the 'corrections' he makes to letters are in fact altering an *already* correct sentence. Yet nobody has the nerve to tell him because it simply isn't the done thing to correct a 'Prince'. So he is allowed to live with this delusion that he speaks wonderful English and nobody else does.

Poor, pathetic Charles. No wonder he thinks the rest of the world is always wrong: after all, isn't he surrounded by people who convince him he is always right? Hasn't he always been surrounded by these people? A former girlfriend of Charles's recently said, 'The amazing thing is that Charles might have lost a lot of public respect, but he lost none of his friends – even when his behaviour was appalling, even when he had cuckolded one of his best friends. Why? Because he is a Prince.' So even his friends, it is clear, don't mention these things. They do him no favours in the long term.

Despite having no recognisable intellect or ability, Charles, scandalously, is accorded a public role and his statements about public policy are taken seriously. Amongst his blatantly political roles (for which he has no qualifications at all) in the last year have been: firstly, his fierce advocacy of vaccination in the foot-and-mouth crisis, which he was able to put to the Prime Minister repeatedly. Why? If an ordinary member of the public, even one who was an expert in the disease unlike the know-nothing Prince, had called the Downing Street switchboard, they would not have got through to Blair. Why was Charles allowed extensive access simply because of who his mother was?

Secondly, Charles is a government 'design tsar', giving him the power to stamp his 'vision' of classic architecture on Britain's new hospitals. This is despite the fact that the Prince's architectural skills are so poor that he was given only a 2:2 in the second part of his degree, which was in this subject. The initiative was, according to an aide quoted in the *Observer*, 'very much his own idea'. (Who else would have thought of him?) 'He will be talking to firms directly', apparently. His earlier forays into the world of architecture have been failures: his plans for an eco-friendly model village in the Hebrides had to be ditched. Yet, surrounded by sycophants, Charles has not got the message that he is too untalented and unintelligent to meddle in this area. No, he meddles on. Charles even had the nerve in December 2001 to accuse architects of having 'inflated egos': the lack of self-knowledge is breathtaking.

Thirdly, the Prince acted as an 'unofficial envoy' during the war on terror. Charles and his spin-doctors were eager to see this task trumpeted in the press (it made the front page of the *Daily Mail*), despite the fact that it was meant to be a behind-the-scenes job. Charles's task was to keep the Saudi royal family – notoriously one of the most corrupt, decadent and totalitarian ruling houses in the world – on side, because he is so friendly with them. Yet even in this, he was unsuccessful: the House of

Saud has publicly distanced itself from the 'war on terror'. Downing Street had to waste its time, at a vital moment when every second counted, listening to Charles whining that he should be found a role, and then finding somewhere to shunt him off to. Far from being helpful, having a brainless Prince blundering around the globe was an unneeded distraction.

This was part of a long and rather desperate attempt by Charles to find a foreign-policy role for himself. He infuriated Margaret Thatcher for one when he conspired inappropriately with the Foreign Office to systematise his relations with the Middle East. Thatcher rightly saw this as an attempt to set up a Foreign Office in miniature without any reference to that tiresome bunch, the democratically elected government. As one Foreign Office civil servant said, when Thatcher found out, 'the sound of breaking furniture could be heard all around Whitehall'. Busy Prime Ministers should not have their carefully rationed time wasted like this. Charles can't, I suppose, be blamed personally for this though: the very institution of monarchy guarantees that he will be surrounded by yes-men who convince him that, simply because of who he is, he has something to contribute.

Fourthly, Charles has a predilection for offering utterly irrelevant personal blueprints. He has in the last year authored articles titled 'My Blue-print for NHS Hospitals' and 'My Vision for Urban Renewal'. He even in the 1980s wrote a book called 'Vision of Britain'. Hasn't anybody told him that Kings and Princes don't have any remit in public policy anymore? It is offensively arrogant for him to assume that simply because of birth, he has the right to offer these 'visions' and expect them to be treated seriously.

But then, we should be aware that Charles believes that the monarchy has a right to be superior to politicians. When he first attended a meeting of the Privy Council, an institution which contains all current and former Cabinet Ministers, he wrote that, 'I daresay many politicians would like to do away with this particular institution and establish something more rational and modern but it is one of the last remaining links between Crown and Parliament and does help to remind Ministers that there is one final authority that is not themselves.'

He thinks, then, that it is a good thing that the people's democratic representatives are reminded of the undemocratic 'final authority' that hangs over them. Similarly, he has said that he 'will not be diverted from using the authority of his position to speak out across a range of public issues'. But what authority does his position have? Why on earth should a hereditary position have any authority at all? The very idea is madness. Charles has often shown that he expects to be treated differently because he is a royal. He insists that politicians call him 'Sir' and 'Your Royal Highness' still. He even believes in a hierarchy within the royal family itself, showing that he believes people are carefully ranked according to birth into a caste-system-style hierarchy (feudalism yet again). He once screamed at his father, 'Don't you realise you are speaking to the next King?'

One small sign of his arrogance is revealing. He was given a list of the rules of the University of Aberystwyth when he was a student there. It said at the bottom, 'His Royal Highness … would comply with the rules and regulations', to which he responded by writing, 'Like hell!' Another can be found if we look at when Jim Callaghan, the Labour Prime Minister, tried to find some meaningful work for Charles in the mid-1970s. Callaghan suggested that Charles take a job in Whitehall or the Cabinet Office, or as a member of the Commonwealth Development Corporation. Charles refused to do the job unless he could enter at the absolute top.

In an interview with Mary Riddell last year, Charles made the extraordinary claim that, 'as usual I am rubbished and ridiculed'. Hello? Does he have no awareness of his own position at all? If it were not for who his mother happened to be, his nonsensical speeches and articles simply wouldn't appear at all. Nobody would publish the articles or turn up to hear the speeches, for he has nothing intelligent or incisive to say. Far from being 'rubbished and ridiculed', he is granted a respect and attention he does not deserve. When Charles delivered one of six prestigious BBC Reith lectures in 1998, he was the sole lecturer not to answer questions at the end. It's clear why: his arguments were so nebulous and often risible that he would have been ripped to shreds. He plainly lacked the intellectual rigour to stand up to cross-examination.

There is nothing wrong with having a low IQ; some of the people I most love in all the world do not have the quality of high intelligence, but have other, wonderful, qualities. What they don't do is delude themselves that they can 'cut it' as intellectuals, and then get all sour and bitter when they aren't treated as such.

But Charles emerges time and again as a man who, hilariously, believes that he is an intellectual prophet who is being ignored by foolish figures like the government. He told Mary Riddell, 'On integrated healthcare, on sustainable agriculture and public private partnerships I have had to battle and battle and battle against a complete wall of opposition.' This opposition comes from 'everyone, everyone. All the professional bodies, the institutions, the media.' This truly is the deafness that comes from only hearing sycophants. Never once does it seem to occur to him that it is not the government, the professional bodies and the media who are wrong, but him. After all, this triumvirate of critics actually takes the trouble to either become elected, work hard for qualifications and expertise, or attract customers, not activities which the unaccountable Prince ever troubles himself with.

He went even further in a speech to the British Medical Association in the 1980s, so arrogant that it defies description. He said – clearly in reference to himself – that, 'Perhaps we [meaning 'I'] just have to accept that it is God's will that the unorthodox individual [that is, me] is doomed to years of frustration, ridicule and failure in order to act out his role in the scheme of things, until his day arrives and mankind [!] is ready to receive his message, which he probably finds hard to explain to himself [that's because you're unintelligent and inarticulate, Charles], but which he knows come from a far deeper source than conscious thought [like Laurens van der Post, perhaps?].'

It might seem cruel to repeat Charles's deranged speeches which imply that he is a Moses-type figure, and it might seem even more cruel to mock them so heartily. But isn't the ultimate cruelty to let him continue in these bizarre delusions without pointing out that everyone is laughing at him? I can only think of those times we've all experienced when you emerge from the dressing room in a clothes shop and say, 'Do I look good in this?' Some friends will say you look fine in order to bolster your feelings in the short term, even if you look hideous. I'd rather be told that I look awful in something because then I won't buy it. In the same way, Charles needs to be told that he isn't Moses leading us to the Promised Land. His true friends aren't the ones who allow him to think that he has discovered some deep underlying truth about the universe that, if only the rest of us were as smart as him, we'd all acknowledge. His true friends should tell him that he simply doesn't have the intellectual calibre to make this kind of speech, and that he should just move on and find something else to do.

However, I wouldn't recommend a career in business. Charles has also showed a crass lack of intelligence in his dealings with the corporate world. *Guardian* journalists Oliver Burkeman and Angelique Chrisafis helpfully chronicled the Prince's idiotic relationship with Spanish tiling firm Porcelanosa. Charles – a man who is a millionaire many times over – accepted a garden worth over £100,000 for his private home at Highgrove. In a blatant reciprocal favour, Charles hosted a lavish corporate party for the firm, and flew over to Spain to supervise the opening of one of their factories. Charles appears to have been too stupid to realise that this would inevitably come to light, or too arrogant to care about the perception that the British monarchy is available for hire despite the fact that its members are paid a massive wage to serve the British people.

Charles appeared not to realise the hypocrisy in his stance when he argued that, in light of the 'Sophiegate' embarrassments, personal business engagements were incompatible with royal status. Sophie Rhys-Jones might well have been tempted to answer his criticisms with two words: Armand Hammer.

Hammer was the elderly chairman of Occidental Petroleum when he first bought Charles. Now, you might think that the head of one of the most polluting oil firms in the world would be an unlikely friend of Charles the self-proclaimed environmentalist and lover of nature, but that would be again to foolishly presume that Charles has any coherence or consistency. (Remember: this is a man who preaches fuel conservation yet drives one of the greatest fuel-wasters in the world, a Bentley – or rather, three of them. This is a man who took a trip to the USA to inspect urban slums and spent half the trip playing polo. This is a man who preaches about agricultural traditionalism but was quite happy to shut down his own 'model farms' so that he could make an extra few quid by 'rationalising' the Duchy of Cornwall. His hypocrisy is so blatant that you have to almost admire his nerve.)

Hammer was keen both to donate large sums to charity and to make it very well known that he had done so. So Charles allowed himself and Diana to be bought for a night by Hammer in return for a donation of one million dollars; they turned up at his ball and gave this weird old crook (who was, oddly, a long-time sympathiser with the totalitarian Soviet Union) a great deal of kudos. Hammer was delighted to be viewed as yet another one of Charles's gurus.

Quite why Charles is so intoxicated by the ultra-wealthy is a mystery. As Prince of Wales he has inherited (or ungratefully accepted from us, the taxpayers: it depends on your perspective) the Duchy of Cornwall, which adds £321 million to his personal fortune. It gives him an annual income in excess of £7 million. This should, of course, be largely considered public income and go back into the tax pot to pay for schools and hospitals. Instead, it is claimed exclusively by one man. He must, admittedly, hold it in trust: Charles must pass it on to the next Prince of Wales, and he cannot touch the Duchy's capital. Who on earth thinks that Charles works sufficiently hard to earn £7 million a year, more than fifty times the wage of the Prime

Minister? The government at the very, very least should claim rightful ownership of the Duchy, use the vast sums it earns to pay for public services, and pay Charles a reasonable wage for the job he does – perhaps £50,000 per year, a little below the rate for a school headmaster.

But taking all the profit from the Duchy – our Duchy – isn't enough for Charles. In 1999, Charles sold 2,500 acres of trees which he claimed to own privately to the Duchy (us). His insistence that he owned this land privately (rather than as part of the Duchy) was rather undermined by the fact that the trees were planted on Duchy land and their maintenance was paid for by the Duchy. Even Duchy officials admit they had no need for the timber. The *Mail on Sunday* argues that this was a devious way to get around the rule that bars the Prince from selling capital assets for his own profit. Not content with the millions he already receives, this supposedly humble Prince wanted an extra few million in the bank.

He clearly sees taking exorbitant amounts of money from the state as his birthright. This greed becomes even more striking when you realise that the Prince is given access to a huge amount of expensive luxuries free of charge. If, for example, he wants a swish holiday abroad, he has more than enough super-rich friends who will lend him premises for nothing. His friend John Lastis (who, as an oil tycoon, is a strange bedfellow for a self-professed environmentalist) has lent Charles his £25 million yacht over ten times since 1991, entirely free of charge. He doesn't even have to pay for his London flat (the British people do) or his transport to official functions (for which British taxpayers stumped out a whopping £1.3 million in 2001).

It would be wrong, however, to say that Charles has not done some good things. Despite his awful, warping upbringing, which has cruelly made him into the grotesque caricature he is today, he has tried to do some good for the poorest people in our society. He has used his privileged access to the wealthy to establish an excellent charity, albeit one rather self-servingly entitled the Prince's Trust. The Trust carries out valuable work day in, day out with some of the most disadvantaged young people in Britain. A friend of mine was given a grant by the Trust to set up his own business, and it turned his life around. Yet even the work this has taken fills Charles with self-pity: he told Riddell that, 'I've tried to make the most of the position I'm now in. If that kills me in the process, then so be it.'

Charles's commitment to charity and the poor is, however, somewhat undermined by his own relentless decadence. This is, of course, an imitation of his grandmother Elizabeth Bowes-Lyon. A palace insider has said that, 'his attitudes are very like hers. He mirrors her view of life.' His grandmother has encouraged him 'to be really royal, in the old style'. When Charles travels, he demands seven bedrooms to himself. This includes a dressing room, a room where he can write his letters, and accommodation for his preposterous number of servants. His staff includes three butlers, four valets, four chefs, ten gardeners, and more. He insists that his staff at Highgrove wear specially designed uniforms and bow to him every day when they first speak to him. The journalist Graham Turner has described Charles's Sandringham parties: 'To start with, there must have been 20 or 30 servants ... Everybody had their own individual valet or maid and, each evening [at dinner] ... jaws dropped open at the splendour of the table, the silver, the decorations, the flowers, the statues and the lighting.'

His mad self-indulgence is occasionally comic. He spent hundreds of thousands of pounds building a garden which he wanted to be 'the outward expression of my inner self'. It is less funny, however, when you realise that he is spending hard-earned taxpayers' money which could be used on schools, hospitals and caring for the elderly. Charles uses £3,000 *a week* of public funds from the Duchy of Cornwall to pay for the upkeep of his partner, Camilla Parker-Bowles, who doesn't perform any public duties at all. Yet his private office provides her with a car, pays her household bills, and splashes out on the upkeep of her horses. He used public RAF jets to take his kids and some friends over to Zurich and then on skiing. His squandering of our money is offensive, to say the least.

Yet it is hard to blame Charles Windsor for his obvious character flaws, because we are always drawn back to admitting that he was appallingly badly brought up. Even now, his parents treat him in a despicable way. At the time of the 'Camillagate' revelations, the Queen was concerned that 'Charles' melancholy and his sense of defeatism would outweigh his sense of duty to the Crown.' This is true cruelty. Your son has been publicly humiliated and ridiculed after a dreadful invasion of privacy, and he entirely understandably becomes deeply depressed and tempted to withdraw. Yet your reaction is to worry not about that but about an inhuman institution. This is the climate in which Charles was raised. Is it any wonder that he is such an odd man?

And now, of course, we must discuss the relationship which is central to his life but which the institution of monarchy prevents from being formalised. The story of Charles and Camilla is actually a very moving love story. The first time they met, Camilla strode towards him and said frankly, 'My great-grandmother was your great-

great-grandfather's mistress. How about it?' From that moment on, they appear to have had a special bond which has endured their marriages to other people and several intervening decades.

Yet they are unable to marry without constantly monitoring grotesque opinion polls, with intrusive findings such as that (in a poll to mark Charles's fiftieth birthday!) 40 per cent believe they should marry and 46 per cent believe they shouldn't. He is also constantly conscious that – uniquely for a man in his fifties – his mother can block his marriage. A senior courtier has explained, 'On this issue, the Head Lady is not for turning. She has rehearsed all the constitutional and legal arguments ... and knows she can block the Prince of Wales from getting married. To her, Charles either becomes king and puts Camilla aside, or marries her and reconsiders his future.'

Confronted with appalling parenting and the distorting effects of monarchy, is it any wonder that Charles is the way he is? What is a little shocking is that Charles doesn't seem aware of the extent of his own freakishness. When Mary

Riddell told him he seems like a very normal dad, he said, in a voice she describes as 'suddenly querulous and huffy', that, 'I don't see why people think I am abnormal.' He has been so abused by monarchy that he can't even see how warped he has become. That, perhaps, is the greatest tragedy of all.

8

Anne, Andrew and Edward

The Spares

Elizabeth Windsor's three youngest children are described by virtually everybody who has met them as spoiled, arrogant and unpleasant. But I believe that we should have sympathy for these three misfits, because they have been raised in circumstances where they could hardly grow to be anything but. They are the product of a Palace culture best described by Charles Maclean, who held the most senior position in Buckingham Palace from 1971 until 1984. He explains that, 'the only rules that royalty obeys are those they make themselves. It's no good trying to judge them by ordinary standards because they simply don't apply ... You can be made to stand and listen to an absolute tirade of abuse even if you are not the guilty party.' Can you understand now how children surrounded by people with this attitude all through their youth would inevitably become warped?

Maclean described it even further: he says that, 'the royal family are not always right, but they are never wrong'. So Edward, for example, has never been told, in candid terms, that he is wrong, that he has no talent in television (or, it seems, any other area). So he has no sense of humility. He views the world through a lens of incomprehension, asking in vain why only those within the Palace circle can see how 'brilliant' he is.

Andrew is another sad example of a royal who, because of deference, has a painfully warped personality. Any normal person who thought it was 'playful' to ram a live lobster down the front of a date's swimming costume would be shunned socially as, bluntly, an arsehole. He would soon learn that his behaviour was idiotic and adjust accordingly. Yet this process through which we all acquire basic social skills sadly hasn't happened with Andrew, because people allowed a royal boy to behave differently. In the long term, this has done him no favours. A friend of Andrew's, Ferdie MacDonald, once asked him why he was constantly throwing things at girls and squirting them with water. Andrew looked puzzled. 'They like it, don't they?'

One time in the early 1990s in Harry's Bar, Andrew interrupted a friend in mid-anecdote by banging his knife on his glass and shouting, 'I want to tell a story! I want to tell a story!' He then waffled on for ten minutes with 'an embarrassing lot of nonsense ... but nobody said anything. He's a Prince.' Edward displays similar symptoms of being socially deformed. He would, for example, instruct his girlfriends on a first date that the proper way to address him was as 'Sir'.

Similarly, Anne has not been taught that her disgraceful rudeness is unacceptable. To give but one example, on a visit to the House of Representatives, she criticised one of the great national symbols, the bald-headed eagle, saying that it was 'a most unfortunate choice'. But perhaps most striking is her comment – surely the most offensive made by any member of her family, or indeed any British public figure – when she described the horrific disease AIDS as 'a self-inflicted wound'.

Anne's attitude towards servants is very revealing about the mindset of the royal children. It shows clearly their view that 'commoners' are deeply inferior to 'royals'. Her very, very sympathetic biographer Brian Hoey asked a bodyguard who often cared for Anne's children whether he was viewed as an uncle. The bodyguard replied, 'Nothing could be further from the truth. I'm just a piece of furniture …. Even as little kids, they never get too close.'

Anne's attitude to Brian Hoey is also revealing. He accompanied her on a four-day tour to Texas. Despite the fact that she knew he was writing a book which did nothing but praise her, she blanked him entirely, refusing to acknowledge his presence even once. Hoey was at first a little put out, until, 'I discovered there was nothing personal in this and that the same rules applied to her personal staff.' A person who ignores entirely those who are working flat-out on her behalf is a person whose character has become deeply flawed. Yet again, monarchy was responsible.

Anne merely reflects an arrogance which extends across her family. Once a servant leaves royal 'service', they cease to exist in the eyes of the Windsor family. They are never contacted again (not so much as a Christmas or birthday card), never invited back for parties, never the recipient of phone calls to see how they're getting on.

A former confidante of Anne has confided that her attitude towards the monarchy approximates that of a number of old-style patrician Tories who have outlined their attitude in the press. Peregrine Worsthorne has expressed it best: what Britain has become is, quite simply, not good enough for the wonderful Windsor family. Once we pity the royal family, the whole idea of monarchy collapses. It devalues monarchy itself and destroys even the memory of the institution. Therefore the only sensible position for a true monarchist now to adopt is republicanism. Anne showed that she believes this when she took flowers from an elderly woman outside the church at Sandringham at Christmas 2000. The 'commoner' asked Anne to pass the flowers to the 'Queen Mother' because she had brought them hundreds of miles specifically for her. Anne snapped: 'What a ridiculous thing to do.' Of course, Anne was right. It was a ridiculous thing to do.

The late Auberon Waugh said, reflecting Anne's view, 'we are no longer a fit country to have a monarchy' and that the Windsors 'should be allowed to return to Germany with dignity and decorum, the plaudits of a grateful people ringing in their ears, and leave the Princess Monster [Diana, who was at the time of writing still alive and very much a rival to the Windsors] behind to receive the cheers of her adulatory fans, Madonna-like, until they grow bored and decide to tear her to pieces.' In a way, of course, he prophesied what did happen to Diana: the Princess was ripped to pieces by the people, or at least the chasing paparazzi collecting photographs of every second of her life on the people's behalf. With an attitude like this to the monarchy, though, it is little wonder that Anne and her siblings behave in an astonishingly arrogant fashion.

In fairness, it can only be pointed out yet again that they were appallingly badly brought up. Their mother, for example, has shown so little care for Anne that when she told Elizabeth that her marriage had irretrievably broken down – a moment surely when maternal love was needed – the monarch simply said, 'I think it's time to walk the dogs', and left.

It should also be pointed out that the monarchy has seriously damaged their romantic lives. For example, Anne had a romance with Andrew Parker-Bowles (who later went on to marry the notorious Camilla). Andrew has admitted that, 'we were terribly fond of each other'. But their relationship could not proceed because Andrew is a Roman Catholic, and – in a gross insult to Britain's Catholics – anybody of that faith is forbidden to marry anybody who is in the line of succession.

A similar tragedy occurred when Andrew began a passionate affair as a twenty-three-year-old man with American actress Koo Stark. He told her he loved her and even mooted marriage. But the tabloids revealed that she had appeared in some soft-core lesbian porn, and she became an embarrassment to the Firm. Despite the fact that he was an adult, Andrew was told by his father that the relationship was over, and he meekly accepted the command. He never spoke to Koo again: another life ruined by monarchy. Andrew was forced to dump his girlfriend on the orders of his mother, despite the fact that he was a grown man. Why, he was entitled to ask, shouldn't a hormonal young man be allowed to have as much consensual sex as he liked? Yet, the *Sunday Mirror* reported in 1984, 'The Queen has made it clear that she will not tolerate any more "indiscreet behaviour"', and that, it seems, was the end of the matter.

Monarchy has made these children so flawed that they cannot have successful marriages. Andrew and Sarah's marriage was wrecked in part by monarchy. Andrew had learned from his mother that Duty to an abstract institution must supersede duty to those trifles like your spouse and children. As a result, he spent most of the early years of their marriage away at sea with the Navy. Sarah would later describe herself as 'abandoned for his job'. But Sarah's friends describe 'Andrew's serious attitude problem' – caused undoubtedly by the monarchy – as the main reason for the breakdown of the marriage. They explain that 'he always wanted to be centre of attention'. Of course he did – he had been raised in an institution which taught him that, because of heredity, he deserved it. Royal children are so cosseted from birth that they will almost always be failed spouses.

It is a sign of how socially maladjusted Andrew was that he chose to marry in the first place a woman who was so weird that she would make her own father curtsy to her. She actually made her aides distribute a memo when she was on foreign trips instructing people not to speak unless spoken to, not to instigate any form of conversation, and to address her as 'Your Royal Highness' and not 'Your Majesty'. Can you imagine the level of a mind that would make such instructions? Can you imagine the level of a mind that would find somebody like that attractive?

Yet the grotesque Sarah Ferguson has also been a victim of monarchy. Like Diana, she felt an intense and cruel pressure to lose weight (she was, in fact, perfectly attractive and the average dress size for a British woman). She began using slimming drugs which impaired her judgement. As Jack Temple, one of the 'healers' she visited, has said, 'slimming drugs fogged her brain. Her actions weren't normal.'

A royal upbringing has also rendered this trio incapable of any meaningful work. Andrew's work colleagues in the Navy found him utterly intolerable. When volunteers were invited to join his helicopter service, not one person stepped forward. He once approached his rear admiral, Nigel Dempster explains, and said, 'You can call me H.' 'And you can call me Sir', he replied curtly.

Edward decided, quite sensibly, to resign from the Royal Marines in 1987. He was far too stupid and ill-disciplined to be part of an intensive and important military attachment, and the idea that because of 'protocol' and 'duty' he should endanger the Army's operational utility was foolish. Yet Edward was subject to a barrage of press criticism and even attacks from his parents for 'letting the family down'.

When Edward went to work for Andrew Lloyd Webber's Really Useful Company – a theatre production company – he insisted that he wanted to be treated just like everyone else – but also let it be known that he expected people to stand when he walked into the room. Edward expected the same kind of deference he received as a royal when he entered the commercial sphere. But, as usual now (thank god), when capitalist sentiments clashed with feudal ones, capitalism prevailed. At a press conference in 1987 to launch his dire TV works, the journalists reacted with the sentiment the documentaries deserved: scorn. He stormed out of the press tent furiously, unable to comprehend – because nobody had ever told him before – that he was talentless, and that the untalented do not have a right to claim praise simply because of who their mother is.

His Ardent TV production company has so obviously cashed in on his royal connections that it doesn't even need reiterating here. Suffice it to say that a random selection of shows his company has produced includes 'Windsor Restored', 'Edward on Edward' and 'Crown and Country'. Who can blame the poor man? He has no other abilities, and he knows no other world. In a properly socially mobile society, Edward would sink down to the bottom of the economic pile, get a job washing cars and probably be quite happy with it. As it is, he can't be allowed to find the kind of menial job that would suit a man of his abilities, so his time is filled with cashing in as best he can on the only even vaguely interesting thing about him.

The main role of that unfortunate couple, Edward and Sophie, is to illustrate that modern business life and monarchy are incompatible. The couple aimed to show that, in addition to their royal 'duties', they could be modern business people, so Sophie refused to quit her job in the PR business when she became a royal. But she underestimated how life-destroying monarchy is: she was soon caught on tape being rather blunt and foolish by a *News of the World* journalist. She described Cherie Blair as 'horrid, absolutely horrid' and William Hague as 'deformed', and clearly used her royal status to draw in the supposed Arab sheikh.

If royals continue to work, embarrassments like this will continue to happen. Of course they will be employed because of their royal credentials: as long as there are stupid and snobbish people who rate royalty, there will be people seeking to profit from it. So the monarchy is caught between a rock and a hard place. It can either become progressively mixed up with business interests, which will make the royals look increasingly greedy and discredit them even further in the eyes of the public. For example, when Sophie was pictured, in her royal capacity, conveniently located in front of a Rover 75 that her firm was paid a quarter of a million pounds to promote, she looked (probably rightly) like she was cashing in on her HRH.

But the alternative is equally horrible. The Firm can insist that none of its members work outside a royal capacity, which will make them all even more purposeless and bored (and prone to self-indulgence) than they already are. Either way, they are doomed to misery. Why not quit while they're behind?

Anne, to be fair, has gone furthest of the Queen's children in distancing herself from the monarchy. Although she still enjoys the lavish and expensive perks of the trade, she has signalled that she doesn't want to be seen as an active member of the Firm by, for example, moving out of royal residences entirely, and renting her own private accommodation.

But all three of them still expect to live in enormous material luxury. It is a sign of how strikingly decadent royal children are raised to be that Andrew, for example, thinks his massive income is inadequate. He receives in excess of £300,000 a year for his royal 'duties' (and he is given a free palace to live in), but he is well known to whine about his finances. Edward and Sophie live in the £10 million property Bagshot House. It is set in eighty-eight acres of parkland. More importantly, Edward uses it to run his TV company. The Civil List shells out in part not only for this massive property but also, then, to subsidise Edward's failed TV career (his company Ardent has lost over £2 million so far).

There are other, smaller cruelties which have been inflicted upon them by monarchy. Thanks to the institution, Andrew has had to live with persistent rumours that Philip Mountbatten is not his real father, but that he is in fact the child of Lord Porchester, the Queen's racing manager. Nigel Dempster told the writer Christopher Hitchens, 'Get a picture of Prince Andrew and then one of Lord Porchester at the same age. You'll see that Prince Philip could never have been Andy's father.'

Given the horrible, weird little lives they have been forced to lead, we can hardly be surprised that Elizabeth's three younger children have turned out to be horrible, weird little people, can we?

9

HARRY

Another Sad Tale

The younger sibling of the heir to the throne is in an exceptionally difficult position, as the miserable life of Margaret Windsor shows. You get all the downside of growing up royal (not seeing the real world, the constant surveillance, the lack of privacy, etc.), but you get few of the perks (power, influence), and you almost always get an inferiority complex the size of Sandringham.

Since he is so much less physically attractive and, by all accounts, less popular and clever than William, Harry has it even harder. Susannah Harvey, a friend of Harry's who is also a model, has revealed his deep feelings of inferiority to William. She explains one occasion when she got a bit tipsy with him and they wandered away from the pub they were in to a field, where they had a snog. She worried that his bodyguards might be looking for him, 'and he said, "I am not the important one." I told him: "Of course you are," but he didn't seem to agree. I got the sense that he felt really insignificant, which is so awful.' She added, 'I got the impression he is perhaps rather unhappy and partying is for him some kind of escape. I feel quite sorry for him.'

Of course, anybody growing up in the isolation ward of monarchy needs escape. Harry, famously, did what virtually every other teenager in Britain enjoys of a weekend: he got ridiculously drunk and smoked a few spliffs. For that, he got labelled for ever in the press and public's minds as 'a drug-taker'. He was even forced by his father, psychotically, to go to a drug rehab clinic (For a few spliffs? Hello? Sanity?). He became the subject of ridiculous moralising articles like one from the *Daily Mail*, which lectured: 'He has, after all, been drinking since he was twelve, and was two years younger than that when he had a "drag" on a cigarette in the company of former royal nanny Tiggy

Legge-Bourke ... Tiggy must look back with great regret on that moment when she foolishly allowed the young prince to try a puff. No-one, of course, is blaming Tiggy for Harry's slide into cannabis use ... If ever a child needed watching, nurturing, guarding and disciplining, it was Harry.' Why on earth should Harry Windsor have been subjected to this madness?

Occasionally his behaviour has, admittedly, crossed a line into plain yobbish unpleasantness. At the Cornish resort of Rock in 1999, he threw cider bottles and screamed abuse at passing girls. One girl who met him at that time was quoted in the press as saying, 'He is the most revolting person I have ever met.' When he was asked to return a pair of skis at the end of a Swiss skiing trip, he threw them at an assistant screaming, 'You take them fucking back.' And at his friend Tiggy's wedding, he swallowed a live goldfish. This is all pretty basic laddish attention-seeking, albeit at the nastier end of the spectrum. It might again demonstrate the malformed social skills that afflict royals though.

Harry, like William, also believes that the press

murdered his mother. He has dealt with the death of his mother differently. While William has become introverted, Harry has become outspoken and attention-seeking. 'Harry has found it much harder to cope with their mum's death, I think', William's friend told me. 'He's much more immature, still like a kid really.' He has certainly been more openly emotional about the death. When Harry saw the flowers left for his mother outside Buckingham Palace, he immediately burst into tears and fell into the arms of Diana's butler, Paul Burrell. In 1999 – two years after her death – he was still prone to burst into tears at his mother's absence from their holiday aboard John Latsis' yacht.

We can only speculate about Harry's reaction to persistent rumours that he is not the child of Charles at all, but rather of James Hewitt. It can hardly be a pleasant rumour to hear about yourself. The response given by defenders of Charles, that Diana and Hewitt didn't meet until two years after Harry's birth, was disproved by *Private Eye*, which showed that they met at a polo match in 1981. Diana herself, in the

'Squidgygate' tapes from 1989, talked about getting pregnant by another man whilst still married to Charles. She tells one of her lovers, 'I don't want to get pregnant ... I watched Eastenders today. One of the main characters had a baby. They thought it was by her husband. It was by another man.' She laughed.

This isn't the only probable source of unhappiness for Harry. He has always found it hard to make friends – like Margaret before him. He was asked if he wanted to bring any friends on his 1999 yachting holiday. William brought along a whole gang of both sexes. Harry brought nobody. The 'revelations' about Harry's very moderate drug use had horrible repercussions for Harry's social life too. Frightfully respectable posh parents were suddenly terrified that their kids would be tarred with his matted royal brush, and Harry found that his jet-setter friends mostly vanished. Harry has always been lonely, and never more so than now. His group of friends has been broader than William's though. The *Mail* stated with horror that, 'Some of [the women Harry mixes with] are very different from the aristo crowd William sees.' Surely not – a Prince mixing with *common folk?* You can almost feel the *Mail* staff collectively shudder.

Harry has been publicly loyal to his friend Guy Pelly, who was incorrectly blamed for leading him towards drugs, in part because he has very few other friends, and in part because he despises the press and wanted to show that he won't be pushed around by them. This point is crucial, because it shows that, when William quits, Harry is not prepared to step into the fray. As my source told me, 'Harry? Christ, he's not going to want the gig when William turns it down. They've discussed it, because William looks out for his younger brother and obviously he knows that the spotlight will switch onto him. They're agreed. Neither of them wants it. They hate the press, they hate what happened to their mother ... When William jumps, Harry's jumping with him.'

The crown could, I suppose, pass to Andrew Windsor. But, really – isn't it time to just call it a day?

Part II

And What Was It All For Anyway?

The Case Against The Monarchy

There are circumstances in which it would be acceptable to sacrifice the happiness of an entire family. Millions of families were made miserable during the Second World War, but it was for the greater good of combating fascism. So, is there a good reason for imprisoning the Windsor family within the institution of monarchy? Has all that misery been for a worthwhile cause?

There are plenty of arguments in defence of the monarchy, many of them proffered by decent and sincere people. One of the most compelling is the view that Britain's constitutional monarchy was a key reason why Britain, unlike the rest of Europe, was able to resist fascism and communism during the twentieth century.

It provided a stable core and focus for our loyalties.

Telegraph editor Charles Moore is the best exponent of this view. He argued in 1994 that, 'when there is the threat of a coup in many African or Latin American countries, for example, everyone asks which side the monarch will be on. In Britain we know the answer to that question: the army is loyal to the monarch, and that is the end of the question.' This seems like a tempting argument. The image of a British monarch who commands the loyalty of his or her people and in turn secures constitutional stability seems attractive.

Except for one crucial fact: in reality, one British monarch had Nazi sympathies, and if he had got his way he would have sold us down the river to Hitler.

Edward VIII said to the editor of the American magazine *Liberty* that, 'it would be a tragic thing for the world if Hitler was overthrown'. He plotted with the Nazis to become King – with Wallis as his Queen – of a Nazi-occupied England. His aristocratic friends, such as the

Mosleys and Metcalfes, are all well known to have been pro-fascist.

An army loyal to him and not to the elected government of the day would have been an army who handed over these islands to Adolf Hitler.

Ah, the monarchists reply, but Edward VIII and his pro-Nazi beliefs never ascended to the throne – thus proving that the system has a built-in check against extremism. This is historical revisionism, pure and simple. Edward was not crowned because he wanted to marry an American divorcee. That is all. If he had restricted his romantic longings for aggressive social climbers like Elizabeth Bowes-Lyon, he would have become King and been free to plot with Hitler from the very heart of the British state as much as he liked. It seems pure luck that he did not. So, far from being a source of stability, the British monarchy brought us perilously close to fascism in the twentieth century; it was, in contrast, the good sense of our people and our elected representatives who resisted it.

Yet still the myth that the monarch provides us with a non-controversial, non-political head of state around whom we can all rally at times of crisis persists. As with so many topics, Winston Churchill has given the most eloquent argument in this area. He argued that one of the main functions of the Crown was that it provided us all with a non-political focal point to which we were all loyal, making it 'the central link in all our modern changing life, the one which above all others claims our allegiance to death'.

Unfortunately, Churchill was wrong, and he knew it. He himself tried to use Elizabeth as a party-political pawn when he tried to schedule the Coronation as close to the general election as possible, because he thought this would bolster support for the Tory Party. The monarchy fundamentally is *not* apolitical. In fact, it is highly political – and the monarch herself is forced to be a highly political creature. Indeed, her former Prime Minister Harold Macmillan said in his autobiography that, far from diminishing in the twentieth century, 'in many ways the royal influence has grown', all the better for being behind closed doors.

David Owen, the former Labour Foreign

Secretary and one-time Prime Ministerial contender, makes this extraordinary admission: 'The fact is that a lot of people in very important jobs feel they serve the Queen and not the Prime Minister [that is, the non-elected rather than the elected part of our constitution], and the Prime Minister knows there is that element in the system. Those people would go to the Queen's private secretary if they thought anything was wrong. The Chief of Defence Staff would not hesitate to talk to her. Not only does the Queen take very seriously the ambassadors and senior military commanders who leave this country for service overseas, but those people very much value their relationship with her.'

This shows how the existence of the monarchy creates a blatantly political tension between the democratic parts of the British constitution and the undemocratic parts. The monarch is expected to keep the democratic parts 'in line'. Unsurprisingly, following Hitchens, this serves the class interests of the wealthy and propertied. Any government which strayed too far from the accepted parameters of the Establishment would be called into line by the fact that the government machine doesn't serve them – the democrats – but the monarch. How much more political can you get?

But this is only the tip of the iceberg. The monarch is given many significant political powers which he or she might be called upon to use at any moment. For example, the monarch has to appoint the Prime Minister. Now, this seems like it has become very straightforward, since by convention the monarch simply appoints the head of whichever party can command a majority in the House of Commons. But occasionally circumstances emerge where it is not obvious which party can do this. This is no hypothesis: it happened in 1974. Following the first general election of that year, Labour Prime Minister Harold Wilson won a small majority in the British constitution's slice of democracy, the House of Commons, but Elizabeth still called on Tory Prime Minister Edward Heath to see if he could form a coalition with the Liberals. This was a highly contentious move. (As it happens, he was unable to form a coalition with the Liberal Party.)

That power remains today. If we had a 'Gore vs. Bush' scenario in Britain, it is the Queen (not, as in the USA, the Supreme Court) who would break the deadlock. William Rees-Mogg, the former editor of *The Times* and bastion of the British establishment, confirms this. He said in this, the Jubilee year, that the Queen retains significant powers to choose the Prime Minister. He said, 'you can conceive of a situation in which ... supposing the three major parties all had exactly the same number of seats ... you would then have to make a judgement about which of the three party leaders had the best chance of securing a reasonably durable majority in the House of Commons ... the Prerogative would still be there.'

The journalist Simon Heffer is a valuable guide to what would happen in this eventuality. (Indeed, he is an extremely useful source of information on the monarchy, partly because he is so sympathetic to them and partly because, barking mad and nauseatingly right-wing though he is, he writes very well.) In 1994 he identified that, if there was a hung parliament, the Queen would receive the advice of constitutional experts and leading figures. Amongst these advisors, there were two Labour supporters and five Tories: an imbalance even greater than that on the Supreme Court. So Elizabeth Windsor embodies a systematic bias in favour of one political party: hardly apolitical.

But that isn't the end of her powers. Oh no. She can refuse a Prime Minister's request for a general election, the absolute focal point of our democracy. Again, this is not some theoretical, it'll-never-happen situation: the question has arisen repeatedly in the last few decades. Tony Benn challenged Martin Charteris, Elizabeth's private secretary, in January 1974 about the rules governing the dissolution of parliament. Charteris told him that 'the Queen has absolute rights'. This question became a highly pertinent one in 1974. Following Heath's failure to form a pact, it was strongly predicted (rightly, as it turned out) that the new Prime Minister, Harold Wilson, would ask Elizabeth for another general election very soon. Many argued publicly that the Queen should refuse any request for a dissolution if it seemed that another election wouldn't break the deadlock or if the other parliamentary parties could join together to form a coalition. She seriously considered this.

Following this fuss, there was an official review into the Queen's powers in this area. Edward Short, who headed the investigation, concluded that 'constitutional lawyers of the highest authority are of the clear opinion that the Sovereign is not in all circumstances bound to grant a Prime Minister's request for dissolution'. Nothing has happened since to change this state of affairs.

Robert Rhodes James, the outstanding historian and constitutional expert, gave a speech in 1990, in which he argued that the Queen's power to refuse a Prime Minister's request for a general election remained very real and highly significant. Many people thought at the height of the poll-tax furore that Thatcher would call a general election to resolve the issue once and for all. Rhodes James said that the Queen should refuse such a request 'in the interests of the nation'. Again, the monarch is shown to be not apolitical but at the very heart of the British nation's politics.

One of her other political functions is that she is guaranteed an hour-long meeting with the Prime Minister every week, and a long weekend at Sandringham with him every year. Charities and businesses would cheerfully spend literally millions to achieve this degree of access. The monarch receives it gratis. And, contrary to the lies told by monarchists, she uses it to lobby for her own political beliefs. Of course she doesn't do this entirely openly. She won't say to a Prime Minister, 'Look, Tony, I'm really pissed orrrrf with the minimum wage.' What she does do is described brilliantly by constitutional historian Ben Pimlott, and it is worth quoting him at length: 'She did not directly criticise the Government's plans. But she measured her response to them. She would often express, or hint at, her own opinion by asking a leading question, or referring to somebody else who had an alternative view. If she approved, she would say so, positively. Disapproval was indicated by a failure to comment.'

She uses this influence to real effect. Lord Armstrong, who worked very closely with Harold Wilson and Edward Heath, has said, 'I know from personal experience that there were at least two Prime Ministers who came away from audiences impressed by what the Queen had said – and taking it seriously.' Several former Cabinet Ministers have described how she uses her power over them too. Geoffrey Howe, the former Chancellor and Foreign Secretary, has (although a monarchist) admitted that all Cabinet Ministers succumb to 'a pervasive aura of deference' when dealing with 'the Queen'. William Waldegrave, the former Tory Cabinet Minister, has explained that, 'She is formidable. I've been shouted down by Mrs Thatcher and it was very unpleasant, but I'd much rather have that than the Queen's disapproval. I wouldn't want to face those eyes and those folded arms.' So a democratically elected Cabinet Minister was *more afraid* of offending the unelected monarch than the elected Prime Minister. This is a serious offence against democracy, and profound evidence that the monarch is a very long way from being 'apolitical'.

Several figures who have seen her work extremely closely confirm this. Henry Kissinger, the murderous former American Secretary of State, agrees, and describes the Queen as 'a very interesting lady with a lot of savvy ... *Far from being the mere figurehead she appears to be*, she also knows a great deal about the electoral system in Britain' [My italics]. One of her former Prime Ministers, James Callaghan, sees her as a political operator, saying earlier this year that she 'has *acute political judgement which sometimes seems at odds with the general public perception of her*' [My italics]. A civil-service advisor to Margaret Thatcher has said that, 'if the Queen offered views on any subject, she would have them taken seriously'.

You don't have to share Tony Benn's hard-left politics to share his indignation at this preposterous deference our democratically elected leaders are forced to display towards this unelected, unrepresentative figure. He described in his diaries the process of being sworn in as a Privy Councillor as 'terribly degrading as we were told to kneel on a footstool before the

Queen'. He was disgusted by 'the attempt to impose tribal magic and personal loyalty on a people whose only real duty was to their electors'. Labour MP Paul Flynn backs up this argument with his account of royal functions. He explains that 'the sad "subjects" assemble hours beforehand and wait. Cattle waiting to be herded are treated more kindly. The sole purpose of this event is to reinforce royalty's delusion of omnipotence by abasing the peasantry before them.'

Former Foreign Secretary David Owen shows the hideous sycophancy that this induces in even Labour Ministers when he says that, 'There's a certain gut loyalty that's difficult to explain. The Queen calls on reserves within all of us. We all go that extra little mile for her.' What, and not those trivial little figures like your electors or the Prime Minister, David? You go the extra mile *for the Queen?*

Many monarchists believe this is a perfectly proper state of affairs. They honestly believe that Elizabeth is superior to Britain's elected leaders. This can be seen in ultra-royalist writer Brian

Hoey's complaint that Tony Blair's 'presidential style of leadership' infuriates royalists, 'who think he considers himself her equal'! Well, heaven forbid that a man who actually takes the trouble of becoming our democratic Prime Minister thinks – oh, the obscenity – that he might be *equal* to this totally undemocratic woman who is our head of state for hereditary reasons. At least we can't accuse the monarchists of hiding their offensive views.

Monarchists respond to factual statements that the monarch has considerable political power by saying, 'well, yes – but Elizabeth Windsor has no political views at all, so how can she lobby for anything?' They then give a self-satisfied laugh and assume they have won the argument.

In fact, they are yet again ignoring the facts and the truth. Elizabeth Windsor has very-firmly-held political beliefs, which creep through into the public domain occasionally. Elizabeth has made a number of broadly philosophical speeches which reveal her political attitudes on social affairs, for example. Early in her reign, she repeatedly launched attacks on 'materialism' – a point which was a bit rich coming from a woman who divided her time between four luxurious palaces.

She revealed her views to be in line with what we would now call the traditionalist right on social issues. She criticised 'growing self-indulgence' and said, 'we can have no doubt that divorce and separation are responsible for some of the darkest evils in our society today'. (Really? And leaving women trapped in violent, abusive or just plain unhappy marriages is just fine and dandy, is it?) No doubt people will respond to my criticisms by saying that I am not judging Elizabeth by the standards of her time. But this argument is fatally flawed. In the time in which she expressed these unpleasant views, Elizabeth was criticised. The Marriage Law Reform Committee, for example, pointed out that Elizabeth was expressing extreme views and before a particularly right-wing and conservative audience, the Mothers' Union.

The court surrounding Elizabeth has long been a bastion of the most regressive and vile social conservatism too. In 1960 – the year that heralded the decade of the Beatles – the snotty old queens who made up the clique of royal courtiers insisted that 'known homosexuals' should not be invited to Margaret Windsor's wedding, in case Elizabeth Windsor was seen to 'approve of their degeneracy'. Even today, unmarried women who work for the Queen, like Heather Colebrook, the Buckingham Palace housekeeper, are given the 'courtesy title' of 'Mrs', because single women are deemed to be socially inferior.

Elizabeth has made a few statements which veer dangerously close to party politics. Her 1983 Christmas message, for example, expressed a number of views which flew in the face of the policies of the government of the day. In blatant defiance of Margaret Thatcher, who for better or worse (I think worse) was the elected Prime Minister, she said that, 'The greatest problem in the world today remains the gap between rich and poor countries, and we shall not begin to close this gap until we hear less about nationalism and more about independence.' The speech then cut away to Elizabeth speaking to Indira

Gandhi, whose socialist government of India was vehemently despised by Thatcher. Now, as it happens I agree with Elizabeth's sentiments in this instance, but that isn't the point. The point is to show that it is a lie to say she is 'above politics': she has often made her political sentiments clear. If we, the British people, disagree with her and what she says, what can we do? We have no mechanism to remove her or express our opposition.

Peregrine Worsthorne, a quintessential Establishment man-about-town, has been one of the shrewdest observers of the personal politics of the monarch. In 1986, he pointed out that Elizabeth's politics reflect those of her (again unelected) courtiers. She used to have aristocratic courtiers who encouraged her to make reactionary speeches like the one to the Mothers' Union. By the 1980s, he suggested, she had 'replaced one unrepresentative and undemocratic lot of sycophants with another', this time a more leftish, pro-Commonwealth group, 'thereby ending up even more isolated in an ivory tower than she has been before'.

Elizabeth's political views burst into public view in 1986 in the *Sunday Times*, in a sequence of events which is still disputed to this day. The affair seems now to have gone something like this: William Heseltine, the Queen's private secretary, gave a series of informal briefings to a *Sunday Times* reporter which he believed were for a long-term article about the monarchy. He got carried away and made public a bit too much of what by convention should have remained private. The picture that emerged from this very close confidante of Elizabeth was that, 'Far from being a straightforward countrywoman ... who is most at ease talking about horses and dogs, the Queen is an astute political infighter who is quite prepared to take on Downing Street when provoked.'

At the time, the left were so happy to find this unusual ally in the Palace (it was reported that the Queen was very worried about inner-city decay and good race relations, for example) that they failed to address the blatant offence against democracy that this involved. The right were reluctant to attack Elizabeth's politics because of their sympathy for the institution of monarchy; so, pretty much, she got away with what should have been revelations to shake the unelected monarchy to its foundations. After all, here was an unelected figure using considerable insider influence to try to shift government policy simply because of her personal prejudices.

This affair focused on Elizabeth Windsor's driving political passion: the Commonwealth. One of her biographers, Roland Flamini, said that, 'God know she's supposed to be above politics, but everyone knows she gets politically involved, especially if it concerns the Commonwealth.' She has fought from her hereditary position in defence of the Commonwealth for decades – often in direct opposition to the view of Britain's elected governments. A.N. Wilson has put it best when he said, 'it is possible that the Queen is the only person in the British Isles who is interested in the British Commonwealth. Most of her subjects have some difficulty in remembering what exactly it is.'

Despite this, she has fought against our democratic leaders for it. Edward Heath, a curiously underrated Prime Minister, had, in the words of one of his biographers, an 'undisguised disrespect' for the Commonwealth. His well-known passion for Europe meant that he had little time for this silly, post-imperial talking shop. Martin Charteris has admitted from the heart of Elizabeth's inner circle that this made her relations with Heath 'very heavy weather'.

Bernard Ingham, Margaret Thatcher's notorious press secretary and one of her closest confidantes during her time in Downing Street, admitted recently that Thatcher and Elizabeth disagreed strongly about the Commonwealth. 'Mrs Thatcher never held the Commonwealth in the same degree of importance or affection as the Queen. Mrs Thatcher thought it to be an expensive luxury with few benefits for Britain', he explained, 'while the Queen obviously regards her position as Head of the Commonwealth as of prime importance.'

Ingham is uncharacteristically being restrained. Thatcher despised Elizabeth's beloved Commonwealth. Whenever the Commonwealth was attacked from a Tory Party Conference platform,

Denis Thatcher would cheer. Carol Thatcher revealed, in her biography of her father, *Below the Parapet*, that Denis and Margaret would curse the institution, and joked that the CHOGM – which stood for the Commonwealth Heads of Government Meeting – was really an abbreviation for 'Coons Holidaying on Government Money'. (What lovely people those Thatchers are.)

Elizabeth Windsor's influence, against these Prime Ministers' clear desire, has actually kept the Commonwealth (a huge drain on the British taxpayer) alive. Vernon Bogdanor, the constitutional expert, argues that, 'It is difficult to imagine the Commonwealth continuing to exist in its present form without the King or Queen as head.' Ben Pimlott goes further and says it is hard to believe it would still exist without Elizabeth herself at its heart.

This is partly because the Commonwealth provides her with some scraps of power and some justification for the continuation of the monarchy. Elizabeth's pompous reaction to the 1983 invasion of Grenada, a small Commonwealth island, reveals that she very much expects to be a key figure in the government of Commonwealth countries, despite being unelected and unaccountable. When the USA invaded the island of Grenada, it didn't cross their minds to call an irrelevant old woman who had scarcely ever been to the island. Elizabeth, however, threw a tantrum, and had her press people inform *The Times* that she was furious.

In defence of these powers over Commonwealth countries, Elizabeth has used all her powers – including, perhaps surprisingly, her sexual ones. When Gough Whitlam became Australian Prime Minister in 1972, he was suspected of having republican sympathies. So Elizabeth Windsor set about trying to convert him. Lord Charteris explained that she went so far as using her sex appeal: 'A lot of her sexuality has been suppressed but, that night, she used it as a weapon. She wrapped Gough Whitlam round her little finger, knocked him sideways. She lay on that rug in front of him, stroked it and said how lovely it was. It was an arrant use of sexuality.'

The monarch's political influence will be even more offensively undemocratic in the unlikely event that Charles Windsor becomes King. What on earth would happen if – in a not unrealistic scenario – he found himself with an anti-organic food, pro-GM, anti-Public–Private Partnership government? Would he use his weekly meetings to lobby the PM with his totally unrepresentative and unchecked (not to mention ill-informed and poorly understood) views? How could any democracy tolerate such an insult?

Indeed, Charles has already used his position completely inappropriately for political influence, as I hope I showed fairly comprehensively earlier. But just to reiterate the point, it's worth bearing in mind that the Prince admitted to his biographer Jonathan Dimbleby that he specifically intervened in disagreements within the Thatcher government in order to press for his own political beliefs and argue against the (democratically elected) Secretary of State, Nicholas Ridley. He used every possible opportunity – including meetings with the Secretary of State and meetings with his ministerial rivals – to lobby in favour of one of his (blatantly political) pet projects. He provoked the normally sanguine Ken Clarke (then Education Secretary) into a fit of rage when he blatantly tried to affect the content of the National Curriculum.

He is such a notorious political in-fighter that Michael Heseltine told him he had 'all the hallmarks of a seasoned politician'. One former Minister, Peter Morrison, has recounted how Charles called him into Kensington Palace and screamed and shouted and banged his fist on the table when Morrison wouldn't accept his arguments.

We therefore have very strong reason to believe that he would try to exert pressure on a Prime Minister in the same way. It will be utterly impossible to maintain the myth that the monarch is apolitical or above politics: our next monarch is unashamedly a political lobbyist with his own highly politicised agenda. He even publicly admitted that, 'I understand the perimeters in which I can operate but at the same time I'm quite prepared to push it here and there because I happen to be one of those people who feel very strongly and deeply about things.' At least we can't say he didn't warn us.

My point here is not to say that he shouldn't talk about politics. Seeking to influence public policy is an admirable desire in any citizen. If, as is clearly the case, Charles wants to do this, he should abdicate and stand for election or try to get a job as a policy advisor or journalist. What he cannot legitimately do in a self-respecting democracy is claim a right of access to those at the highest levels of government simply because of who his mother is.

Charles tried, when he was a student, to get involved in politics. He asked the master of his college, Rab Butler, if he could join the Labour, Conservative and Marxist parties, hoping that the overlapping memberships would cancel out any accusation of political bias. Butler refused permission. Of course, if Charles abdicated, he could join any party he wished.

It is worth pointing out that, just as the monarch tries (and future monarchs will try) to use politicians, so politicians often try to use the monarch. Ben Pimlott describes eloquently the first such occasion in Elizabeth's reign, when as Heir Presumptive she was sent on a tour of Northern Ireland where she was a blatant political tool in the Loyalist battles against the Republicans. He describes how an 'almost hysterical atmosphere of loyalism' accompanied the tour. The pattern of using Elizabeth has continued intermittently. She was similarly manipulated by Harold Macmillan into selecting his preferred candidate to succeed him as Prime Minister, an episode which even devoted monarchists now acknowledge to have been a serious misjudgement on the Queen's part.

Despite all this, some monarchists still argue, ridiculously, that Elizabeth Windsor and her heir are apolitical. Look: Elizabeth does two hours of government paperwork *a day*. What do these monarchists think this paperwork is? They cannot have it both ways. They cannot say on the one hand that the monarchy has no power and is purely decorative, yet on the other hand laud the Queen's incredibly hard work on constitutional matters. Only one of these compliments can be true.

The arguments that we have a 'non-political' head of state are utterly discredited. The oldest defence of monarchy can be found in the argument that the monarch is imbued with special powers by God. He or she has a divine right to hold the throne, and his or her presence enshrines the vital place of religion at the heart of the nation's identity.

Surely, you're probably thinking, nobody believes that nonsense any more. But religious justifications for the Crown underlie many arguments about the monarchy, and they are – extraordinarily – believed by the Windsor family themselves.

Margaret Windsor told A.N. Wilson seriously that her sister Elizabeth 'is God's representative in this realm'. Dr Geoffrey Fisher, the Archbishop of Canterbury who 'crowned' Elizabeth, argued – in terms so inappropriate for a Churchman that they surely border on idolatry and blasphemy – that 'on Coronation day, this country and the Commonwealth were not far from the kingdom of heaven'. He described the Queen as 'God-called', and said that the

Coronation ceremony called her 'into the presence of the living God'. This sounds extremely similar to the Divine Right of Kings. A significant slice of the British people accepted it too. A poll in 1953 found that three in ten Britons believed that Elizabeth Windsor could claim direct descent from God.

I don't sneer at these people, and nor should you. My grandmother, who is one of the best human beings in the world, might well have been part of that third of the British people. There was compelling propaganda which seemed to support this view. People who cleaned toilets (as my granny did) really were encouraged to believe that 'their betters' had a closer connection to the divine than common folk like themselves.

Of course, these were the original justifications for absolutist monarchies. The early English Kings claimed they were direct descendants of Woden, the Anglo-Saxon god of war. Victorian constitutional writer Walter Bagehot, who is considered the ultimate authority on the British monarchy, wrote that, 'If you ask the immense majority of the Queen's subjects by what right she rules, they would never tell you that she rules by parliamentary right ... They will say she rules by "God's grace": they believe they have a mystic obligation to obey her.'

John Stokes, the then Tory MP, was still arguing that Elizabeth Windsor was closer to God than her subjects in the 1990s. He said that the ultimate reason the Queen was given greater respect than politicians was because 'we remember that the Queen was anointed and crowned at her coronation and therefore is a quasi-religious person'. The author Sue Townsend has explained that when she was a child in the 1940s – when John Stokes was also being educated – kids were 'still being taught that they [the royals] were God's representatives on earth, and I really believed that the Royal family could cure leprosy'.

The author Fay Weldon still believes, curiously, that a religious air clings to anything royal. She explained recently (and apparently seriously) that, 'The words Royal Mail make it feel somewhat treasonable to rob a mail train; years later we find ourselves still talking about the Great Train Robbery.'

To be honest, I find it difficult to argue with people who expound these views. It's like what happens when an atheist tries to talk round somebody who believes in God: it's impossible. And if people choose to believe the utter madness of Divine Right, then who are we to stop them? All we can point out is that Britain is now predominantly an irreligious country (only 7 per cent of the population go to church every Sunday, with a further 1 per cent attending mosques, synagogues and temples), so any justification for monarchy on religious grounds has crossed over into outright defence of theocracy. They can say what they like – but the British people are laughing at them.

Related to the religious arguments is the view that the monarchy must be preserved because it embodies Tradition. Often, this is a simple secularisation of the religious arguments: the monarch is endowed with a special role not by God but by History, and therefore he or she is beyond challenge by us mere mortals.

The British monarchy, they argue, contains deeply embodied (and often not immediately apparent) wisdom which has lasted for millennia, and it is the height of human arrogance to think that we can rationally replace it with our own haphazard creation.

Again, Charles Moore gives the best account of this view. He says that the monarchy embodies 'the wisdom of the ages', and those who seek to overthrow it 'exhibit that peculiar frivolity which characterises a certain sort of clever person, the pernicious quality that Michael Oakeshott called rationalism'.

A reasonable-sounding Burkean argument can be made that institutions which have evolved over many hundreds of years do indeed embody truths and knowledge which we cannot rationally apprehend and will not truly appreciate until they are gone. But this argument is entirely specious. If we adopted this view, we would never have demolished any feudal institutions, and most of us would still be serfs working for the feudal lord of the manor. It was 'rational' to demolish these, and indeed Oakeshottians rather undermine their own argument by creating a rational argument against rationalism.

Furthermore, it simply isn't possible to argue that the monarchy as it currently exists has evolved across the ages. Almost every aspect of the monarchy which anyone in this country comprehends was invented from the air in the last 150 years. It is not 'the wisdom of millennia' which gives us the monarchy but the haphazard improvisation of a couple of country squires and wacky aristocrats who devised new ways of putting on a royal show.

Steven Haseler, the distinguished politics professor, has shown how the justifications for the monarchy have been created over the last century. In the 1870s, the country's courtier class decided to revive the monarchy by associating the royal family with nineteenth-century imperialism. This is how the lavish, ceremonial monarch was created: not through the wisdom of the ages, but through a couple of blokes not that long ago having a brainwave and seeing if it worked. Similarly, the disastrous idea of a monarchy focusing on fetishisation of the family was created when the imperial monarchy became untenable. And so on: there is no deeply buried, barely visible wisdom here. Conservative thinkers like Moore have a vested interest in arguing that the monarchy is deeply mysterious and ancient. It is not. It is easily comprehensible and, as we understand it today, a recent invention.

So, it appears that Moore's argument is based on a fundamental misunderstanding of the nature of monarchy. Almost all the monarchy's 'traditions' were invented very recently. For example, royal weddings have only in the mid-twentieth century become a source of excitement and palaver. They are the brainchild of the notorious Elizabeth Bowes-Lyon. Charles Windsor was subjected to an 'investiture' ceremony as Prince of Wales. This was invested with mock-religious overtones in his 'oath', and all the pageantry and expense associated with royalty. Yet it had scarcely any historical precedent at all. There had only been one earlier ceremony, which was the 1911 investiture of then-Prince Edward. Almost all royal traditions, when you study them, crumble into dust of very recent provenance if you look closely. To give but one more example, Elizabeth Bowes-Lyon invented the tradition that private conversations with members of the royal family must not be repeated.

So, it is impossible to defend a centuries-old British monarchy because we don't have one. The monarchy we do have was invented in the last century. Any wisdom it might embody dates only from then.

Intimately related to this misconception is the often-heard argument that the British constitution is a fragile thing. We have a constitution as described by Walter Bagehot, the legendary nineteenth-century constitutional writer, and it works perfectly well, they argue – so why meddle with it?

When discussing the monarchy, constitutionalists always refer back to Walter Bagehot, as though his say-so closes an argument. I have had similar experiences with Americans who simply refer back to their own Constitution without ever asking if that Constitution might actually be wrong. This is an especially silly state of affairs in Britain, since one of Bagehot's key arguments was that Britain's unwritten organic constitution was strong precisely because it was free to evolve. To try therefore to preserve Bagehot's descriptions of the monarch's role in aspic, and refer back to it as a quasi-divine authority, is idiotic. Bagehot was perfectly prepared to accept that the constitution would evolve in ways he couldn't imagine – and one of those ways is, today, a legitimate desire to get rid of the monarchy.

Most of what Bagehot said about the monarchy has already been discarded in practice. For example, he said that we must not 'let light in' on the monarchy by over-exposing royals to the public glare. This was given up in the 1960s and would be completely unpractical in a twenty-four-seven media age.

But still Elizabeth Windsor, her son Charles and their foolish advisors and supporters refer back to the Bagehotian 'rights' of the monarch, as if they were, by being described by so venerable a source, self-evident. The monarch Bagehot outlined was one who scorned the 'credulous masses' and had to trick them with smoke and mirrors into reverence. It is hardly a model which even the most ardent monarchist can defend today. Yet study of Bagehot can be very revealing about the true role of the monarchy. We owe to the excellent Christopher Hitchens a reading of Bagehot which puts class interests at its heart. Bagehot was unashamed in arguing that the Crown was an additional insurance to protect men and women of property from the vile masses who have nothing. This small part of Bagehot's analysis is crucial. Bagehot was wrong about many things but he successfully identified why a large proportion of those with power have loyally defended the monarchy even when it defied their own purported ideologies.

As it happens, Bagehot was wrong anyway in his descriptions of the monarchy of his day. He claimed that the monarchy only warned and advised the Prime Minister; in fact, as historians have conclusively shown, the then-monarch, Queen Victoria, exercised far, far more power than that. Robert Rhodes James maintained correctly until his death in the 1990s that the monarch remained an independent source of power within the British system of government; she was not, he explained, merely a force who could influence the parliamentary government.

So, really, those who argue that tinkering with a Bagehotian constitution is dangerous are ignorant of Bagehot himself, and the nature of the British constitution. Oh, and as for the idea that the British constitution works fine as it is: tell that to William Windsor.

One of the recently invented royal traditions which demonstrates the constructed and recent nature of the monarchy is the practice of the royal family travelling around the country opening hospitals, schools and other good national services. As they do this, monarchists argue, they raise public morale. They host many private functions which fulfil the same role. This invented tradition has itself become one of the leading arguments in defence of monarchy.

For Christ's sake, let's be honest about this particular argument for once. Elizabeth Windsor hates hospitals. One of her ladies-in-waiting told Graham Turner, 'I've heard her say, "Why are we going to another hospital?" I'm afraid she's not as good with the sick as the non-sick. She prefers people who are very, very healthy and, since she is hugely physically strong herself, it's much harder for her to get alongside someone who isn't well.' This shows in her hospital visits, which are stilted and where she looks distinctly uncomfortable. Far from raising their morale, these visits often embarrass the individuals involved.

Indeed, Graham Turner has demolished the case that Elizabeth Windsor's public functions spread joy and happiness. This is all the more revealing because he was writing for the ultra-monarchist *Daily Telegraph*, who rigorously check any facts which reflect badly on the monarchy. He describes one Buckingham Palace lunch which sounds positively painful. Elizabeth entered, approached two women, and said literally nothing. Every question or attempt at small talk was greeted with a monosyllabic answer that was openly rude. For most of the lunch she didn't say anything at all, and one guest noted 'the unmistakable unfriendliness'. Eventually she just walked out, not bidding anyone farewell. The guest thought that perhaps Elizabeth was just having a bad day, but Turner was told by a Master of the Household that 'that experience is not untypical'. This is the ugly side of the monarchy which almost always goes unreported. It shows that this vital case for the monarchy – that it cheers people up when they interact with the sovereign – is simply factually wrong. Many, many times, the monarch depresses people by being so rude.

The idea that we can rally around the royal family at times of disaster also no longer holds with reality. When a serious disaster occurs, we look now to the Prime Minister. Margaret Thatcher was the first on the scene at Lockerbie; Major and Blair travelled together to Dunblane; on 11 September 2001, it would have been bizarre if news coverage had cut away to a statement by Elizabeth Windsor. When royals have headed for disaster zones, they have been an embarrassment. Philip Mountbatten told grieving residents at Lockerbie, 'People usually say that after a fire it is the water damage that is the worst. We are still trying to dry out Windsor Castle.' Footage of Charles Windsor visiting the site of the Warrington bomb is just painful. He approached a woman whose leg had been blasted off and told her that she had 'made my day'. Neither he nor his mother spread goodwill – they spread embarrassment.

This argument will then, as the press is more honest about the royals, go the same way as the now defunct argument that the royal family provide us with a moral example.

In the 'post-toe-sucking era', we don't hear much about this any more, and rightly so. But it's important to register that this was *the* argument for the monarchy for much of the twentieth century. As late as the early 1980s, the writer Rebecca West wrote in *Time* magazine that, 'The Royal scene is a presentation of ourselves behaving well; if anyone is being honoured [by a royal wedding] it is the human race.'

The hubristic notion that the royals should be exemplary moral beings originated with Elizabeth Bowes-Lyon. She held it till her death. When the 'Camillagate' tapes were published (revealing, unsurprisingly, that like everyone else in Britain, Charles talks dirty to the woman he loves), the 'Queen Mother' told him that 'if a man is born a Prince, he must be credited with a kind of moral stature'. When she was 'Queen', she authorised hilarious, preposterous books with titles like *The Family Life of Queen Elizabeth*. Her daughter and son-in-law learned from this. The Queen expected and accepted praise like that offered by the Lord Mayor of London, when he said that, 'Through the medium of television, you have allowed us to look into your uncurtained windows more freely than any generation before.' How fortunate that she had long since trained herself to keep a straight face when confronted with the utterly hilarious. Victoria, the 'Queen' who gave her name to an era, promised voluntarily at the start of her reign, 'I will be good.' Every monarch after Elizabeth Bowes-Lyon had her way was *required* to make that pledge.

Elizabeth Windsor has been keen to cash in on this argument for the monarchy too. Dermot Morrah, a Palace favourite, argued in the 1950s that the Queen's 'exemplary family' was at the absolute heart of what monarchy is about. Following this view, Dorothy Laird argued that 'so much has a happy family life become identified with the British royal family that it is doubtful whether a sovereign could sustain his sovereignty were this shattered'. Yet all the time that the Palace was encouraging these beliefs, the family at its heart were neglecting their children, shagging other people, and lying through their gold-capped teeth about setting 'an example to the Commonwealth'.

It is now clear that Elizabeth and Philip themselves took blatant advantage of the meek British press in the 1950s through to the 1980s to present an entirely dishonest view of their family life. All the time that Elizabeth and Philip were (with painful hubris) boasting of their unity as a family and their role as a 'moral example to the nation', reports abounded of Philip's friendships with other women and of how their poor, desperate children had been virtually abandoned as babies and left for huge periods without any parental contact at all. The 1950s propaganda of their family life was an unashamed lie, and when they learn this, the British public become understandably angry. The Queen boasted in 1972 of her 'happy and united family', an outrageous deceit, and even sought to lecture others on how to have as happy a marriage as her own tumultuous relationship with Philip. We were being taken for fools by a family who were fleecing us for millions. Is it any wonder that an opinion poll in 1998 found that 57 per cent of young British people distrusted the royal family? (We can only marvel at the gullible 43 per cent.)

The traditionalist right is the group most disillusioned with the fall from moral grace of the younger royals. Former *Spectator* editor Alexander Chancellor has asked, 'Is there any aspect of the Windsor family, with its broken marriages and its burning palaces, which can still be held up to Britain as an example of how things ought to be?' To be fair, I don't see how the Windsors can be blamed for the burning of Windsor Palace – unless Chancellor knows something the rest of us don't – but the very fact that this ardent monarchist is so disheartened is very revealing.

The journalist T.E. Utley, who is a guru to many on the conservative right, very eloquently explained in 1987 the consequences of the collapse of the royal family's perceived moral superiority. He said that, 'The royals are there to supply a perennial pageant of virtue – the virtues of family life, of civic disobedience, of respect for the arts, of care for the poor and afflicted.' Without this, the whole exercise of monarchy, he believed, becomes pointless. He said that 'if the present ridiculous exercise continues' – a reference to the antics of the younger royals – then the whole institution may as well be wound up. Since the public failings of the royals will continue to be publicised (both because the press isn't going back into a box, and the Windsor family are like all of us fallible), within the terms of the conservatives who dominated the monarchical debate for so long, the institution is dying every day.

For the rest of us, it can only add to the belief that the institution of monarchy makes entirely unreasonable and cruel demands upon the individuals who happen to comprise the royal family.

It used to be said that, by being raised within the monarchy, royals would naturally be more virtuous. This has plainly proved to be false.

Some still argue, however, that monarchs are 'raised' to be more wise than the rest of us.

This does not correlate with reality. The present 'Queen', for example, was deliberately raised to be unintelligent and uninformed. There was a fear that a 'blue-stocking heir' would present a bad image to a country sceptical of bright women, so her education was severely restricted. She never attended school, and Marian Crawford was horrified by the children's ignorance. When Elizabeth was ten years old, she was only tutored for seven and a half hours a week. The monarch before her was, unashamedly, very stupid. When George VI was a naval cadet at Osborne, he came last in his class of sixty-eight in his final exams. The monarch after her, if it is Charles, will be profoundly unintelligent too.

You cannot raise somebody to be a good head of state, because by the time the child has grown, the very idea of what makes a good head of state might have changed entirely. Fifty years ago, a head of state was meant to embody values which were then seen as 'British' – reserve, stiff upper lip, and so on. So Elizabeth was raised that way. But now we want a monarch who is empathetic, and can weep on cue and hugs sick babies – basically, we want a Diana. But if we raised a monarch who had all those qualities now, what if values shift again and we want something totally different in fifty years? The whole idea just falls apart when you look at it practically.

Another argument offered by monarchists is that the royal family do extensive amounts of work for charity. It is true that some members of the Windsor family do great work for charity – Anne Windsor, for example, has been commendably active in her work on behalf of Save the Children. They could continue to do this work as private individuals in the Republic of Britain. They are celebrities, and celebrities draw in money for charity. In a republic, there will still be celebrities. The USA has a far higher rate of charitable giving, and no monarchy. It has created its own, non-hereditary celebrities.

To retain an entire constitution just to indirectly help charities would be madness – we could, instead, give all the money we spend on the monarchy directly to charity if we wished. This would be far more beneficial to charity and have none of the massive drawbacks of the monarchy. As Paul Flynn, the Labour MP, puts it, 'it is not the royals who are selflessly shoring up the charities, it is the charities who are shoring up a dying institution'.

The arguments seem to be thinning out now; but there are more. The royal family travel the world promoting British trade, it is argued, and therefore earn their money back many times over. They project a confident and attractive image of Britain to the rest of the world.

It is indeed true that occasionally when they are abroad the royal family promote specific business projects associated with Britain. Of course, with a highly fluid global economy it is very hard to delineate what constitutes a 'British' company, and most big businesses are hard to pin down to any one nation. But, still, the royals do their best.

Or do they? Recently declassified documents have revealed that, far from promoting British interests, Philip Mountbatten was so ill behaved and rude on one pro-business trip (the only one so far for which documents are available) that he nearly scuppered a British business deal worth millions. As the documents for subsequent trips drip-drip into the public domain over the next few years, I fully expect that there will be more examples of Philip directly damaging our commercial interests.

As commercial markets become increasingly competitive and the monarchy is increasingly seen as a ridiculous anachronism, though, their ability to really influence commercial decisions is rapidly becoming negligible. The idea that hard-nosed ultra-capitalist businessmen are going to decide to invest in a particular country because Elizabeth Windsor had a nice cup of tea with them is ridiculous. Profit margins will outweigh any fringe royal coaxing every time.

There is a wider question, also, about whether we want to be seen as the kind of Britain which sends miserable aristocrats dressed in ancient crowns and tiaras to do our dirty work. Do we really want to be seen as a country embodied by a desperately unhappy old woman with no social skills who has only ever known the world of the aristocracy? Surely we need to get away from being seen as some kind of heritage theme park writ large?

None of these arguments in defence of the monarchy stand up to scrutiny for long, then. They are not sufficiently strong to justify wrecking the lives of the Windsors for ever. And even on top of them, there remain some other pressing reasons for us to get rid of the monarchy.

Not least, there is the astronomical cost of the whole institution. The right-wing press are very keen to point out the cost to the 'cash-strapped' British people of asylum seekers (which is negligible, especially since we give them virtually nothing to live on and house them in the worst accommodation in the country). They are mysteriously less eager to point out quite how much the monarchy snatches from the public purse.

Elizabeth Windsor receives not only the huge Civil List (worth a whopping £8 million a year), but also (deep breath) the Grants-in-Aid for the upkeep of her Palaces, including the ones which the public are never allowed to see (this costs us £15 million a year), the Royal Travel Grant-in-Aid which covers her personal flights and those of her family (another £8 million), the Royal Train (another cool million), the eight limousines we pay for her to own, the proceeds from the Privy Purse which has been passed from monarch to monarch since 1399 but properly belongs to we, the people (this brought in the piffling sum of £80 million last year), the profits from the Duchy of Cornwall's property (£8 million) ... Do you need me to go on, or do you accept now that the Queen is not some spendthrift little rural lady who leads a simple, Spartan life?

There are also a huge number of hidden costs which don't figure in the normal newspaper calculations. For example, whenever the Queen is on a foreign trip, she charges all her expenses while she is in that country to the relevant British Embassy. His bill includes the cost of the clothes she wears, the clothes her relatives and senior servants wear, and any number of miscellaneous items. The Foreign Office pays these massive bills without questioning them. It is through accounting fiddles like this that the Windsor family drain far more cash from the taxpayer than appears on the Civil List.

There are other wads of cash which need to be factored in. Elizabeth receives gifts constantly from foreign governments and private individuals. The Windsors do not pass them on to the nation to be viewed in museums, schools, hospitals or other public places. They pocket these gifts for themselves. Elizabeth and Philip received gifts worth £2 million *in 1950s money* when they got married, and they hoard these treasures entirely for themselves. On just one visit to the Gulf States in 1992, to pluck a random example, Elizabeth was given carpets worth over £2 million (from a corrupt regime whose people are mainly illiterate and hungry). Surely a republican settlement could allow them to live for the rest of their lives in great comfort simply off the proceeds of these gifts alone?

Then there's the cost of housing the royals. We, the people, own Buckingham Palace, Windsor Castle and Holyroodhouse, but our government gives them rent-free to the sovereign for her entire life. We also pay for the entire upkeep, including electricity bills. The Queen personally owns Sandringham and Balmoral, which she inherited from her father. The value of these two massive properties has not been officially released, but it clearly runs into many, many millions. They are more than ample for ten families, never mind one. In fact, Elizabeth is so astronomically privately rich that she could afford to build a £5 million property for her son Andrew as a wedding gift, and can even buy her sister's ex a £70,000 London town house as a 'divorce present'. Quite why we need to subsidise her accommodation at all is mysterious.

Is there a single person reading this book who isn't able to think of better things to spend these huge sums of money on?

Another argument for slaying the beast is that we are putting the royal family in considerable physical danger by retaining the monarchy.

The Windsors have been physically attacked several times. The Queen, for example, was shot at six times in June 1981, albeit with what turned out to be blanks. The next year, an intruder, Michael Fagin, managed to break into Elizabeth's bedroom. It is pure luck that he wasn't armed and dangerous. Charles was shot at too, in Australia, and Anne was very nearly killed by a gunman who planned to hold her hostage for a £3 million ransom. Charles was threatened as a student by extreme Welsh nationalists, and William was the target of anthrax-attack threats by hardcore Scottish nationalists. Sooner or later, one of them will be killed. Christopher Hitchens has said that by keeping the monarchy we are asking for a human sacrifice. This may be more than metaphor. The monarchists claim to love the Windsors – but they are massively increasing the odds of them being murdered. I'm not sure I'd want these people loving me ...

There are some people who join the condemnation of the British monarchy, but argue that we could stop short of abolition by adopting a 'Scandinavian-style' monarchy. This would, they argue, make the royals more 'normal'.

This is a pipe dream. The very fact that they are raised as royal, and therefore quite apart from anything approaching normality, guarantees that they can never be anything but extremely abnormal people. The scaled-down monarchies on the European continent are often cited as an example, but they have all the same problems as us. Their royals are exposed to appalling media intrusion into their everyday lives, and they still suffer the character-deforming effects of constant boot-licking.

One of the best arguments for outright abolition is that the monarchy encourages the British people to take completely the wrong approach to how power should flow in a democracy. Jonathan Freedland, in his outstanding book *Bring Home the Revolution*, puts this argument brilliantly, and much better than I'm about to. The British psychology about power has always been disfigured by the monarchy. The democratic aspects of our constitution are the bits which have been oh-so-kindly conceded by those at the top. Power is therefore seen as something which flows down from above, rather than something which flows upwards from we, the people. We don't see the government as 'ours' – it is the Queen's. All of our public institutions are not our collective property but 'Her Majesty's'. This has prevented the development of a healthy, empowering democratic culture in Britain. Our national identity has monarchy at its core: we all sing 'God Save the Queen'. Yet a positive, constructive national identity would not put obeisance to the rich aristocracy but democracy at its heart. It is long overdue that the British people reclaim their head of state; the state belongs to us, not 'the Queen'.

Furthermore, the monarchy symbolises entrenched class privilege, one of the great blights on British society. The royals are symbols of one of Britain's most shameful facts: the lack of class mobility which we still suffer from. Born upper-class and rich, there is no doubt that the royals will die upper-class and rich, no matter how incompetent and unintelligent they are. And, no matter how bright and brilliant a poor boy or girl might be, they can never rise to their exalted status. This is the England we all hoped that time would forget, but, no, there it is, hobbling its way into the twenty-first century. How long? How long must we sing this song? (As U2 might sing …)

PART III

AND WHAT'S THE ALTERNATIVE?

A Guide to Slaying the Beast

Every time the monarchy becomes unpopular, the Tory newspapers run scare stories with headlines like, 'Dale Winton To Be President If Monarchy Goes, Poll Finds'. The British people, the papers proclaim, are so stupid that they would elect somebody 'unsuitable' for the job. Tom Utley, the *Daily Telegraph* commentator, has written that he has nightmares about 'President Mowlam waving her wig at the crowds'.

No other constitutional system works, they proclaim. Countries with democratic presidents are a disaster. But they ignore the fact that to our left (in Ireland) and down below (in Germany) we have two outstanding examples of how a president chosen as a figurehead can inspire public confidence, act as a compelling international face for their nation, and cost considerably less than the monarchy too. Indeed, it would be a great honour if Britain ever had a head of state as remarkable and inspirational as Mary Robinson, the former President of the Republic of Ireland.

However, I would not propose an elected president for Britain. Admittedly, there are plenty of figures who would make outstanding Presidents: Mo Mowlam, Betty Boothroyd, Ken Clarke, Paddy Ashdown and Roy Jenkins all spring to mind. But we already have a figure in our constitution to whom the job of head of state could be painlessly and seamlessly transferred. That person is the Speaker of the House of Commons.

In 1971, the House of Commons Select Committee investigating the Civil List outlined the Queen's official duties. It is the closest thing we have to a job description for the monarch. It outlined the four main aspects of her job. Let's look at whether these could be performed better (and far more cheaply, and with much less cruelty) by the Speaker.

(1) Work arising from the normal operations of government, involving the receipt of information and the signing of documents

It is an offence against democracy that this role is performed by an entirely undemocratic figure anyway. The Speaker could very easily be the final rubber-stamp for legislation in exactly the way that the Queen's signature is now. This would involve no constitutional disruption at all. It would in fact entrench the sovereignty of parliament – something the right claim they care about but entirely abandon when it comes to the question of the monarchy.

(2) Receiving a 'large number of important people privately', including in this category Privy Councils and Investitures

What possible good do these meetings do at the moment? They waste the time of important people, who are very busy and could be talking to somebody who actually is there because of merit. Anybody of true importance who is passing through these islands whose work pertains to government meets a Foreign Office Minister or the Prime Minister anyway. So the Speaker wouldn't need to meet them. This function can just be quietly dropped.

(3) Attending State occasions such as the Opening of Parliament, as well as visiting public services or important national occasions

In practice, the Prime Minister conducts many 'public service/national interest' visits, and *his* visits can actually make a difference. For example, when he visits, say, India, he can learn things which will affect foreign policy and international development agendas. Elizabeth Windsor, in contrast, can only smile and wave. As for the 'State occasions', these could all be run by the Speaker as a supreme symbol of our democracy. He or she should open parliament.

(4) State visits, both as host and tourist

The Prime Minister conducts many foreign trips, and receives all important foreign dignitaries.

What does the Queen add to this, other than an additional load of expenses?

So, it is quite clear that the Speaker could perform these minimal duties. This would incur absolutely no extra expense, because the Speaker already has an official residence in the Palace of Westminster, and he already has a substantial wage. So we save tens of millions which we can spend on hospitals, and we show the world that we are a proud democracy into the bargain.

We need to lay the ground for these arguments now, so that when William announces that he will not take the throne, we have ready alternatives to hand. In this day and age, we should be able to reach a political consensus, from both left and right, that it is no longer sensible to torture the Windsor family in this way.

The left is already overwhelmingly republican. Tony Blair has been keen to portray himself as a monarchist, even giving a dreadful speech in which he praised Elizabeth Windsor as 'the best of British'. He stands in a long line of Labour

Prime Ministers who made a point of displaying their sycophancy to the monarch, from Ramsay MacDonald to Harold Wilson (who even said he would postpone his retirement 'if the Queen needs me').

But Cherie Blair is well known to be a republican, and sensibly refuses to curtsy to Elizabeth. Alistair Campbell, Blair's closest political confidante, is a republican. And Tony's government has paved the way for abolishing the monarchy by abolishing the ridiculous hereditary peers from the House of Lords. It's hard to imagine either of Blair's likely successors, David Blunkett or Gordon Brown, sucking up to the monarchy – their indifference to the issue is plain. Most Labour Cabinet Ministers admit that they have republican sympathies once they leave office: Mo Mowlam is only the most recent example. Most Labour MPs, too, will privately admit they are republicans. At a parliamentary debate to offer praise to the 'Queen Mother' on her hundredth birthday, not a single one of over 400 Labour MPs spoke.

The main party of the left and centre-left would,

then, happily follow a leader who proposed to abolish the monarchy.

And we are beginning to hear dissidents on the right who are formulating what a right-wing anti-monarchy script might sound like. The neo-liberal right clings fanatically to the rhetoric of equality of opportunity (which has also been appropriated, with a different meaning and more substantial content, by New Labour). This necessarily involves a distaste for unearned wealth and anybody with status symbols which are not derived from success within the market. The always-thoughtful journalist and former Tory MP Matthew Parris has written in *The Times* that 'royalty in Britain asks us ... to show deference where there is no honest basis. Royalty, placed at the apex of aristocracy, legitimises habits of deference to qualities other than merit. Royalty in Britain is the single most potent symbol of class, and all the unfairness and all the waste of human potential that goes with it.'

Norman Tebbit, the far-right Tory Lord and high priest of Thatcherism, is known for his dislike of Charles Windsor, and this may well become outright republicanism should Charles ever take the throne. After one of Charles's speeches about the unemployed, Tebbit said, 'I suppose the Prince of Wales feels extra sympathy towards those who've got no job because in a way he's got no job, and he's prohibited from having a job until he inherits the throne ... He's forty, yet he's not been able to take responsibility for anything, and I think that's really his problem.' It is impossible to imagine the generation of Tory MPs preceding Tebbit ever making such stringent (or indeed, any) criticism of the heir to the throne. The next generation on may be even more emboldened.

Already, the man who is probably the most powerful figure on the British right (indeed, one of the most powerful men in Britain, full stop) has strong republican sympathies. Rupert Murdoch has several times publicly stated his opposition to the monarchy and said that it holds up the 'flexibility' of British society. As an Australian and a hardcore free-marketeer, his contempt for non-market-based inherited positions is clear. Where he leads, the rest of the right may follow. Sooner or later, the moment will be propitious for the right to agree with us, and then the monarchy will be decapitated once and for all.

There might seem to be a tone of relish in that sentence, but if so, it is a false impression. This has been a sad and depressing book to write. I have had to pore over the wasted lives of an entire family who should have been given the chance to succeed or fail like the rest of us.

Sometimes my descriptions might have seemed cruel. I hope I have avoided what playwright David Hare described very well in 1993 when he said that 'newspapers, led by the Murdoch group, have begun the project of putting the Royal Family in such a state of tension that their lives will become unliveable ... We shall mock them "till they wish they had never been born."'

That is not my intention. Rather, it has been to show that it is cruel to force this poor, damaged family to tour an increasingly hostile country waving feebly until they die, at which point their children will have to take their place on that grotesque miserable-go-round. It's time we set the Windsors free.

Teiresias, the blind prophet, told Oedipus that 'the curse that corrupts the Kingdom is You'. We need now to reverse this. The curse that corrupts the Windsor family is the very idea of a Kingdom. It has made them surrounded by people who, by indulging their every whim, have destroyed their personalities, possibly for ever. All we can do now is apologise profoundly to the Windsor family for the damage we have done to them, and ensure that no child is ever again mistreated in this way. God save the Windsors – and all other families – from the cruel institution of monarchy.

Select Bibliography

I have drawn heavily on secondary sources in researching this book.

By far the best serious tome on Elizabeth Windsor and the monarchy is **Ben Pimlott's** ***The Queen: Elizabeth II and the Monarchy***, which has been republished this year in a Golden Jubilee edition. His writing is intelligent, crisp and manages to chart both the personal life of Elizabeth and the political context in which she operates. It is an absolutely invaluable source. **Sarah Bradford's** ***Elizabeth*** is also useful. **Brian Hoey**'s biography of Elizabeth Windsor, ***Fifty Regal Years***, is as critical of its subject as its title makes it sound. It is nonetheless an excellent source of information which, coming from such a pro-monarchist source, is actually all the more useful in demonstrating the case that the Windsors are psychologically and socially deformed.

A.N. Wilson's ***The Rise and Fall of the House of Windsor*** is irresistibly bitchy and full of readable polemic. The best low-brow work on the Windsors is **Kitty Kelley**'s delicious ***The Royals***, which, ludicrously, isn't available in Britain. However, you can order it from the USA via the Net (amazon.com won't ship it to Britain – ridiculous, I know – but www.barnesandnoble.com will) or you can find it in good second-hand bookshops quite easily. She has all the best gossip, clearly presented, and writes well.

Graham Turner's series of articles over the last few years on the Queen, the Queen Mother and Prince Philip are like master classes in good newspaper profile writing. They can be read at www.telegraph.co.uk. **Christopher Andersen's** ***Diana's Boys*** is full of fascinating information about William and Harry, while ***William: King for the Twenty-First Century*** by **Nicholas Davies** (updated to be ***William: The Rebel Prince***) isn't a bad second choice. **Jonathan**

Dimbleby's biography of *Charles* is surprisingly badly written. Dimbleby has no ear for language and much of the book falls flat. It is, sadly, also far too sycophantic. Yet, Dimbleby's access to Charles means that it still has some interesting information.

Other readable if trashy works include **Nigel Dempster** and **Peter Evans**' *Behind Palace Doors*, **Andrew Morton**'s ground-breaking *Diana: Her True Story*, **Marian Crawford**'s *The Little Princesses* and **Noel Botham**'s *Margaret: The Untold Story*. **Woodrow Wyatt's diaries** (all three volumes of them) contain some startling revelations about Elizabeth Bowes-Lyon. They are even more revealing about the mind-numbingly sycophantic attitude which the royals encourage.

The best serious constitutional works about the monarchy are the writings (in various publications) of those two gurus, **Vernon Bogdanor** and **Peter Hennessy**. I can't recommend enough **Jonathan Freedland**'s *Bring Home the Revolution*. Although I'm not a fan, many people find **Tom Nairn**'s *The Enchanted Glass* a good analysis of the monarchy. Another worthwhile serious read is **A Spirit Undaunted**, by Robert Rhodes James.

The best collection of writing about the monarchy is *The Power and the Throne: The Monarchy Debate*, which is now sadly out of print – but, if Vintage have any sense, it will be reissued for the Jubilee.

Acknowledgements

All through writing this book, I've been reminded that I have been extraordinarily lucky with my teachers, and although I can't thank them all here, I would especially like to praise Jacquie Grice, my wonderful, brilliant A-level politics teacher who fired my enthusiasm for the subject and first got me thinking about the monarchy and a million other political issues; my other teachers at Woodhouse College and King's College, Cambridge, especially Graham Wallace, Sue Roach, David Kinder, and Roger Kirkham; and the people who have been teaching me how to be a journalist, most notably my brilliant editor at the *New Statesman* Peter Wilby, his deputy Cristina Odone and the lovely

Jackie Ashley. I have also been greatly encouraged by some of my journalistic heroes who have been equally generous with their time: I'm thinking particularly of Jonathan Freedland, Julie Burchill, and David Aaronovich. Christopher Hitchens was extraordinarily generous in looking at the manuscript and giving detailed and extremely helpful feedback.

I'd also like to thank my friends, who have listened to me whinge about not being able to finish this book in time a million times in the weeks it was being written, and are wonderful at all times, in all places and at all things. I would like to thank in particular Roseanne Levene, Sarah Punshon, Yael Lackmaker, Anna Powell-Smith, Chris Wilkinson, Adam Seddon, Alex Reed, Tom Akehurst and Hannah Mackay: without them I would have lost my mind long ago.

In case of difficulty in obtaining any Icon title through normal channels, books can be purchased through BOOKPOST.

Tel: + 44 (0)1624 836000
Fax: + 44 (0)1624 837033
E-mail: bookshop@enterprise.net
www.bookpost.co.uk

Please quote 'Ref: Faber' when placing your order.

If you require further assistance, please contact:
info@iconbooks.co.uk